They Changed the World
Inventions, Ideas, and People

by Delana Heidrich

illustrated by Milton Hall

cover by Linda Pierce

Publisher
Instructional Fair • TS Denison
Grand Rapids, Michigan 49544

ISBN: 1-56822-900-3
They Changed the World
Copyright © 2000 by Instructional Fair Group
a Tribune Education Company
3195 Wilson Avenue NW
Grand Rapids, Michigan 49544

Table of Contents

Introduction

Imagine a world with no glass products: no glass jars, no glass plates or drinkware, no glass test tubes or equipment parts, no glass windows, no glass picture frames, and no glass figurines on your fireplace mantle. Now imagine a world with no phonetic alphabet. Crude drawings symbolize limited nouns and verbs, but children do not learn the alphabet, scholars do not read books, and letters do not get combined into new words as society and technology evolve. Finally, imagine the probable state of the world today had Elvis and the Beatles never introduced Rock and Roll or Roosevelt, Stalin, and Churchill not decided to stop Hitler in his tracks.

Inventions, discoveries, innovations, and famous personalities are all intriguing, but some are more than that. Some actually change the course of history! *They Changed the World* introduces intermediate and middle school students to 38 inventions, ideas, and people who changed the fabric of society. Students learn how plastic was invented accidentally and that the Theory of Relativity was introduced by a man who failed high school math. They discover how the invention of gunpowder, the concept of inalienable rights, and the life of Mikhail Gorbachev each affected significant societal change.

Lessons presented in this book are completely self-contained and may be completed by students without teacher assistance. Each invention, idea, and person is presented in a concise, single-page reading followed by two or three activities designed to challenge students to interact with the lesson's material. Most activities can be completed without the use of any outside materials, and no project requires students to look further than basic reference materials, such as dictionaries and encyclopedias.

Assign the lessons individually as homework or extra credit projects; create three complete social studies packets on inventions, ideas, and people who changed the world; or use the lessons to teach reading comprehension to language arts students.

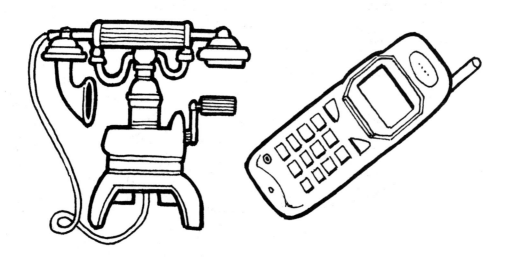

INVENTIONS THAT CHANGED THE WORLD

INVENTIONS THAT CHANGED THE WORLD

Glass

When melted, it can be molded into vessels, pulled into threads, or smoothed into sheets. When cooled, it can provide you with a drinking glass, insulate your house, or help your near-sighted sister see things far away. Yet drop it on the floor, and it shatters into thousands of useless, sharp-edged, skin-cutting pieces.

Glass is an odd substance that is neither a solid nor a liquid. It is found in nature in the states of obsidian and tektite. Synthetic glass was first made in Egypt before the year 3000 B.C. by melting silica found in sand, flint, and quartz at high temperatures.

Humankind has found numerous functional and ornamental uses for glass through the ages. First used only as a glaze for stone and pottery beads, glass was being used to create hollow vessels by 1500 B.C. when Egypt was a thriving civilization. With the Phoenician invention of glassblowing around 50 B.C., glass became easy and inexpensive to make. By the height of the Roman Empire, it was used to create everything from elaborately tooled and patterned ornamental jewelry to everyday tableware. During the Medieval and Renaissance periods it was used to create colorful and intricate stained glass designs and enormous mosaic murals for churches and cathedrals throughout Europe. By the fifteenth century, Venetians were blowing fine, colored glass called *cristallo* into ornamental and useful forms that would be imitated throughout the world. With the rise of the Industrial Revolution during the early nineteenth century and improved manufacturing techniques, glass found more and more practical uses. Today glass products have expanded into every arena in the lives of people worldwide.

How important are glass products in your life? List here every glass product you come in contact with in a typical day: _____

_____

_____

_____

Reflecting on Glass

Silica is combined with other ingredients to create different glasses to be used for different purposes. Glass with large amounts of soda and lime is suited for the production of bottles and lightbulbs and for use as a fireproofing agent and sealant. Silica mixed with potassium and lead oxide creates a heavy glass that can refract light, making it perfect for lenses and prisms. Glass containing borax can stand up to chemical attacks and high temperatures and is used in chemical processing equipment and laboratory glassware. Match the glass types on the left with the facts and definitions on the right. The first one has been done for you.

__C__ 1. Pyrex

A. The high melting point and optical transparency of this "pure" glass that contains nothing but silica makes it perfect for telescope mirrors and heat-resistant containers.

_____ 2. Wire Glass

B. Transparent plastic laminated between two thin sheets of glass makes such items as windshields safe.

_____ 3. Double Glazing Cells

C. Resistance to thermal and chemical shock makes this glass a good choice for cook and laboratory ware.

_____ 4. Fused Silica

D. Most modern-day glass of this type is made by floating large sheets of glass on a continuous bed of molten tin as it cools slowly into a smooth, flat surface.

_____ 5. Plate and Window Glass

E. In the molten stage, wire mesh is introduced into this glass to create strength.

_____ 6. Safety Glass
(i.e. windshields)

F. This glass that darkens in the light is used in printing and reproduction, electronics, and light-sensitive glasses.

_____ 7. Photosensitive Glass

G. This glass is used to make cookware, figurines that are painted as craft projects, and space shuttle tiles.

_____ 8. Glass Fibers

H. These threads or fibers of glass are used in insulation and upholstery material.

_____ 9. Fiber Optics

I. These two sheets of glass sealed at the edges are used as insulators and seals.

_____ 10. Glass Ceramics

J. These glass optical fibers are used for the transmission of images in communications systems.

Shaping Up

How glass is mixed, melted, cooled, and shaped depends on the ingredients that have been added to the glass batch and the glass products to be created out of the batch. Determine the order in which the glass-shaping procedures below were invented by paying attention to the hints embedded in the definition of each method. Make your guesses in the spaces provided. The first one has been done for you.

_____ Old Style Glass Rolling: Beginning in the late 1600s, molten glass was poured onto a casting table and pressed into sheets with an iron roller as it cooled.

_____ Glass Blowing: One of the earliest methods of shaping glass involved rolling molten glass into a small ball to be placed on the end of a pipe and blown and shaped with tongs and paddles. Later, a blowing machine replaced the hand-blown glass-making process.

__1__ Casting: As early as 3000 B.C., molten glass was poured into a mold and allowed to cool. Much later centrifugal casting forced glass against the sides of a quickly spinning mold.

_____ Core Technique: In this technique used over 1,000 years before glass blowing, clay was formed into the desired internal shape of an object to be made with glass and then either dipped into molten glass or wound with glass threads to form the object.

_____ Pressing: Islamic artisans were the first to use simple hand presses to push molten glass into the sides of molds from the eighth to fourteenth centuries. The first mechanical glass press was used in the 1800s. When using a press, both the mold and the plunger can be patterned to create designs on the glass.

_____ Crown Process: Fifteen hundred years before the invention of glass rolling, sheet glass was formed by blowing a glob of glass, flattening it into a disk, and cutting it into panes after slowly cooling it.

_____ Pilkington's Process (New Style Rolling): This glass-shaping technique, first attempted in the 1950s, floats glass on a bed of molten metal and slowly cools it into a smooth, flat surface.

_____ Drawing: Starting at the beginning of the twentieth century, glass was drawn directly out of hot furnaces in sheets to be ground and polished by automatic machines, or in cylinders that could be formed into tubing, fibers, or rods.

The Rocket

Early in the thirteenth century, the Chinese discovered that if they packed gunpowder into a cardboard tube and lit a fuse, the resulting backward expulsion of gases would cause the cylinder to move forward. The rocket was born. First used to launch arrows, carry explosives, and set fires to tents and ship riggings during wars, the rocket has since found a wide range of additional uses.

Launching Satellites: The Russian K. E. Tsiolkovsky first suggested that rockets could be used to push objects into space way back in 1903, but serious attempts at space travel were not made until the end of World War II in 1945. On October 4, 1957, a Soviet rocket launched *Sputnik*, which orbited the earth as its first artificial satellite. Today, satellites that circle the earth serve humankind in a number of ways. Communications satellites provide straight paths for radio waves, enabling transmission of television programs and telephone calls from one side of the globe to the other. Satellite photographs assist in weather forecasting; the assessment of crop, forest, ocean, and ozone layer conditions; map making; and military spying. Signals from the satellite-based Global Positioning System (GPS) help ships and aircraft pinpoint their locations.

Launching Probes: In addition to satellites that orbit the earth, rockets are also used to launch probes that explore—and even land on—other celestial bodies. On July 20, 1969, Neil Armstrong walked on the moon. Since then manned and unmanned probes have explored planets, moons, and asteroids, solving many of the mysteries of our solar system. At first missions of curiosity, today space travel to other worlds is considered essential by some scientists who insist that the survival of our species depends on our future colonization of space.

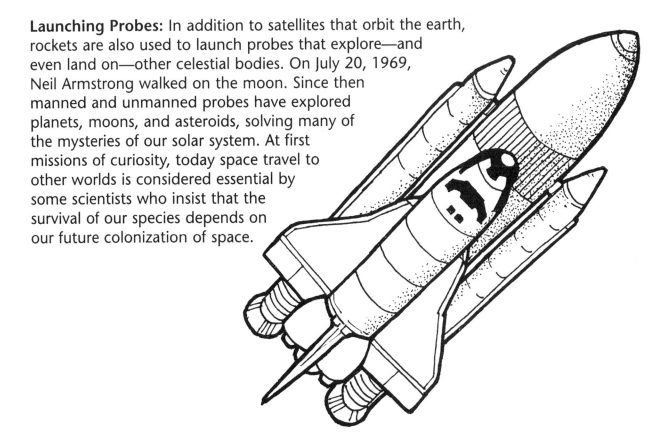

Launching Shuttles and Constructing Space Stations: Booster rockets are used today to launch shuttles, or reusable spacecraft. These shuttles make it possible for new satellites to be put in place, old satellites to be repaired, scientific research projects to be conducted, and space stations to be constructed. Today, 15 countries work together on a 43-flight assembly plan intended to create an international space station for civilian and scientific use. Japan even plans on creating a space hotel. As a U.S. senator, Lyndon Baines Johnson predicted in a 1958 address to the United Nations General Assembly that "Men who have worked together to reach the stars are not likely to descend together into the depths of war and desolation."

Launching Nuclear Warheads: Unfortunately, Senator Johnson may have been mistaken. Rockets continue to play a modern role in destruction. By 1944 Germany had devised a rocket powerful enough to bomb downtown London. Today both bombs and rockets are inconceivably more powerful than they were during World War II. Rockets and guided missiles of all sizes, including those carrying multiple warheads aimed at separate targets, can be launched from ground, air, or water. International attempts at controlling the proliferation of such weapons have been underway since 1946 when Bernard Baruch went before the UN Atomic Energy Commission and called for the abolition of all nuclear weapons.

Which role of rockets do you think is most important to our modern world? Why?

_____

_____

Do you believe human beings will ever use their knowledge of rockets to transport people and equipment to the moon or Mars to create permanent settlements? Why or why not?

_____

_____

Blast Off!

The principle of a rocket motor is based on Newton's third law of motion that states that for every action there is an equal and opposite reaction. When a closed container is filled with compressed gas and the gas is let out a hole at the bottom of the container, the container itself is pushed upward. The Chinese witnessed this phenomenon 450 years before Newton explained it in 1687. Since then, the rocket has advanced considerably. Research one of the rocket achievements listed below and draw a picture of the rocket you study in the square provided. Display your artwork with the work of other students in chronological order to create a pictorial time line of the development of rockets.

1200s—Gunpowder-powered rockets are used by the Chinese as weapons.
1600s—The Chinese use rocket-arrow launchers in wars.
1800s—Congreve rockets are used to carry explosives in wars.
1926—Robert H. Goddard sends up the first liquid-fueled rocket.
1931 —Johannes Winkler launches his HW-1 Rocket (The Fly).
1945—The Germans use the V-2 Rocket—a guided missile—in war.
1945-present—Rockets of all sizes are perfected to deliver warheads and guide missiles.
1968—The Saturn 1B Booster launches the first manned *Apollo* flight.
1969—The Saturn 5, the biggest rocket ever built, carries the first Americans to the moon.
1973—The space station Skylab is launched.
1980s—Solid rocket boosters launch space shuttle flights.
1997—The Pathfinder rover, Sojourner, is delivered to Mars.

_____

Rocket Title and Date of Achievement

The Clock

"The movie starts at seven-fifteen." "He ran the race in 14.72 seconds." Humankind has always been interested in the passage of time, but the accuracy of our clocks and watches today has transformed us into a society obsessed with time.

In prehistory, duration could only be determined by noting the relative positioning of celestial bodies. As early as 3500 B.C., the Egyptians were looking to the shadow cast by a vertical post called a *sundial.* Hourglasses, water clocks, and the burning rates of knotted ropes and marked candles were also popular timekeeping devises. By the thirteenth century, mechanical clocks began to replace these methods, using a weight or spring to power a one-handed instrument that indicated time only to the nearest quarter hour.

Technological advancements and the standardization of units of time have led to greater accuracy in today's clocks and watches. A battery-operated liquid crystal display watch gets the typical student to school on time, and atomic clocks—used in science—can lose as little as one second per one million years.

Modern society depends on the precision of timepieces and the standardization of time. Time zones, first introduced in 1883 to avoid the confusion caused by trains transporting passengers to towns using their own local time systems, are now an integral part of our global community. Stop watches and precision time clocks play an important role in monitoring sporting events. Television programs begin when advertised to begin. And arriving late for an important interview or meeting can mean losing a job or a sale.

How might our society run differently if clocks were suddenly abolished?

_____

_____

What are the disadvantages of adhering to strict timetables in daily life?

_____

_____

I'm Sorry! Did I Wake You?

Modern communication and transportation systems have made the world a single global village. Exchange students, business representatives, and tourists call and travel all over the world every day. Understanding how to use an international time zones map can ensure business and pleasure are conducted at times when acquaintances from around the world are at least awake! Practice reading the map below by answering the questions that follow.

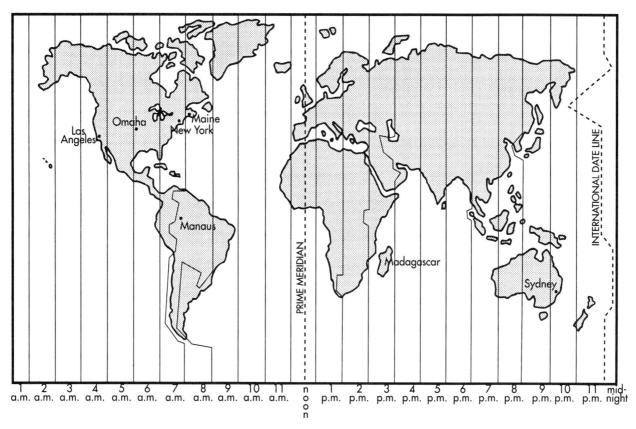

1. It is 1:00 p.m. in New York where you sit in your office and realize you need to call an investor who lives in Sydney, Australia, about a new development. Is this a good time to call? _____

2. Your Omaha, Nebraska, phone just rang. It is your roommate from college calling from his home in Madagascar to tell you that precisely two minutes ago, at 10:00 p.m. his time, he proposed to his girlfriend. Did he wake you up with his news?

   _____

3. Last year you and your other Maine friends enjoyed having an exchange student from Brazil in your class. You tell one of your classmates that you have been missing the exchange student and are going to give him a call in his hometown of Manaus as soon as you get home from school. Your classmate says not to call in the afternoon because it will be the middle of the night in Manaus. Is your classmate right?

   _____

Keeping Time

Several independent innovations in clock-making culminated in the precision timepieces we are accustomed to using today. Match the innovations listed in the box below with their descriptions that follow. The first one has been done for you.

Innovations in Clock-Making

Water Clock	Pillar and Scroll Clock	Pendulum
Coiled Springs	Graham's Deadbeat	Atomic Clock
Liquid Crystal Display	Chronographs	Electric Clocks
Quartz-Crystal Clock	Light-Emitting Diode	Mechanical Clock

Graham's Deadbeat 1. Still used in precision clocks today, this 1715 invention named for the inventor reduces interference in the swing of a pendulum.

_____ 2. These specialized precision timepieces include the pulsometer that graphs a pulse rate and the common stopwatch.

_____ 3. Used as a power source since 1450, these springs were greatly improved with innovations in centuries to follow.

_____ 4. This ancient method of keeping time relied on a calibrated container that leaked water through a small hole.

_____ 5. This extremely accurate clock is important to science.

_____ 6. The mechanics of this clock include a weight or spring, a balance wheel, and escapement mechanisms or gears.

_____ 7. In the 1880s Eli Terry of the United States patented this shelf clock that only needed winding once a day.

_____ 8. This battery-operated wristwatch first produced in the 1970s displays numbers using liquid crystals.

_____ 9. These clocks, used in most homes today, are powered by an alternating current delivered at the rate of 60 cycles per second.

_____ 10. This object that swings back and forth with gravity was first introduced by Christiaan Huygens of Holland as a regulator in weight-driven clocks. It continues to operate as such in grandfather clocks today.

_____ 11. Light-producing semi-conductors display a digital time on this battery-operated wristwatch first produced in the 1960s.

_____ 12. This clock, developed in 1929, connects a ring of quartz to an electrical circuit; it is accurate to the degree of approximately plus or minus one second in ten years.

INVENTIONS THAT CHANGED THE WORLD

Gunpowder

Gunpowder, a mixture of potassium nitrate, charcoal, and sulfur, was first used by the Chinese as early as A.D. 1000 in grenades, bombs, and fireworks. The first written formula for gunpowder was discovered in the 1242 journal of the English monk, Roger Bacon. Firearms and gunpowder were being manufactured throughout Europe by the 1300s. They were instrumental in the destruction of the feudal system when castle walls became vulnerable to cannon balls, and professional men-at-arms replaced serfs in battles between their lords.

Gunpowder use today is limited to fireworks and igniter and artillery shell primer since ammunition for firearms is now made of smokeless, moisture-free wood cellulose. Yet the invention of gunpowder some one thousand years ago led to the manufacturing and perfecting of rifles, revolvers, shotguns, handguns, cannons, and machine guns.

In America today, there exist an estimated 235 million firearms. Intended for protection, hunting, police and military use, or recreational target practice, they have killed presidents and senators, drug lords and CEOs, grandparents and school children. Guns have been the subject of bills and acts and laws that regulate their sale and use. They are the topic of debate during political campaigns, social reform lectures, and public and private conversation. Although they have answered the concerns of how to hunt food, protect family members, and defend nations, the questions raised by the presence of guns in our world may outnumber the answers they provide.

How would the world be different if gunpowder had never been invented?_____

_____

_____

_____

It's Up to You

Many of the questions raised by the presence of guns are questions of opinion that have no right or wrong answer. Use the questions that follow to assist you in formulating your own opinions about issues pertaining to firearms. Record your thoughts in complete sentences in the spaces provided.

1. The National Rifle Association argues that any control over the sale or possession of guns in America is a violation of the Second Amendment that guarantees U.S. citizens the right to bear arms. Do you agree with the NRA's position?

   _____

   _____

2. Proponents of gun control laws suggest that the Second Amendment never intended to place assault rifles in the hands of the clinically insane or to prevent the passage of gun licensing laws. Do you agree with this aspect of the argument made by gun control proponents?

   _____

   _____

3. In many industrialized nations, police officers do not carry guns. Would this work in the United States? Why or why not?

   _____

   _____

4. Following a number of juvenile crimes involving guns in the 1990s, including the tragedy at Littleton, Colorado, some politicians today suggest a law that requires all guns to be sold with trigger locks. Would you like to see such a law passed? Would such a law be likely to keep guns out of the hands of children? Why or why not?

   _____

   _____

5. Does extensive media coverage of sensational gun crime stories make it appear that the United States has a bigger problem with crimes involving guns than it really does have?

   _____

   _____

6. Is it realistic to think the United States could pass a law banning all private ownership of guns? Why or why not?

   _____

   _____

Ka-boom!

Until the 1600s gunpowder was the only explosive known to humankind. Today various types of explosives are employed to achieve military and civilian goals. Choose which category of explosives listed below is used for each of the nondestructive purposes described on this page. The first one has been done for you. You will use each letter more than once.

A. Internal Combustion Engines   B. Small, Controlled Explosions
C. Propellant Explosives   D. Detonating Explosions

__D__ 1. Underground miners use dynamite in the course of mining minerals.

_____ 2. Rocket-propelled fireworks entertain United States citizens across the country on the Fourth of July.

_____ 3. Dynamite is used to clear obstructions to widen a road.

_____ 4. An explosion inside a cylinder pushes out a piston that rotates a crank that turns the engine to power cars and ships.

_____ 5. Diamond dust, necessary for the operation of industrial grinders, is produced from graphite through the use of this mini-explosion.

_____ 6. A rocket propels a communications satellite into orbit.

_____ 7. Metals are pressed into dies or welded together using this mini-explosion.

_____ 8. A new tunnel is created with the use of TNT.

_____ 9. This mini-explosion is used to create a new metal alloy.

_____ 10. Dynamite crushes stones in a quarry to be used in construction and industry.

_____ 11. The principles of jet propulsion allow an aircraft to get off the ground.

_____ 12. Diesel fuel is delivered to combustion chambers where it is ignited, creating explosions that result in the operating of an engine that carries a semi-truck full of groceries to your local market.

The Printing Press

Learn about the invention of the printing press and other means of reproducing words and pictures as you place the inventions described below in chronological order to complete the time line. The first one has been done for you.

Johannes Gutenberg's Printing Press: Generally considered the first printing press, this 1450 invention made use of movable metal letters and numbers that were arranged on a tray to create a desired text before being inked and pressed on paper to create multiple copies.

Signet Stones: As early as 2000 B.C. these seals and stamps cast in clay or stone were dabbed into pigment or mud to make impressions of signatures and religious symbols on smooth surfaces.

Steam-Powered Press: Thanks to the Industrial Revolution of the early nineteenth century, this innovation and others in the printing industry (including the cylinder press, the rotary press, and a press that could print on both sides of the paper at once) considerably increased the efficiency of reproducing text.

Web-Fed Newspaper Press: Patented by William A. Bullock in 1863 and perfected eight years later by Richard March Hoe, this press that printed on rolls rather than sheets of paper made it possible to produce as many as 18,000 newspapers per hour.

Wood Block Printing: The Chinese cut pictures and symbols into blocks of wood to reproduce texts centuries before the invention of the printing press.

Typesetting Machine: Following the 1886 invention of this machine, type could be set by a machine rather than by hand, considerably reducing the time required to prepare for the printing of a text.

Desktop Publishing: Since the late 1970s, computers and specialized programs have assisted individuals in selecting font types and sizes and creating images and text that can be printed on a printer or sent directly to a typesetting machine.

Phototypesetting Machine: This machine that came in to use in 1950 utilizes photographic images instead of metal movable type to create lithographic plates for the reproduction of text.

Printing Press Innovations Time Line

2000 B.C.　　150 A.D.　　1450 Johannes Gutenberg's Printing Press　　1814　　1863　　1886　　1950　　1978

Name _____

The Printed Word

Before the invention of the printing press, any time a person wanted a copy of anything, he/she had to rewrite it! So there were no newspapers, no T-shirts bearing words, or clocks with numbers printed on them. Locate 15 items that have words or numbers printed on them in the following story about the morning adventures of Jennifer Heff. The first one has been done for you.

Jennifer Heff read the back of her cereal box instead of the newspaper as she ate her breakfast. One glance at the calendar on the wall reminded her about the report due in history class today. She better print off that last page she finished writing the night before. With a few pushes of the buttons on her keyboard, Jennifer's computer printer produced a great-looking page of type and images. Jennifer reached for the paper and her binder full of other schoolwork, returned the encyclopedia that she had left out to its place on the shelf, and grabbed the library book that needed to be taken back to school. Then she flung her favorite sweatshirt over her shoulder (the one with the words "No Way" on the back), slapped her Creatures from Space poster for good luck, and ran out the door. She hopped into her beat-up Toyota that was covered in bumper stickers and raced right through the stop sign at the corner and into the school parking lot beside the curb stenciled with the words "Principal Parking." Mr. Baker wouldn't mind if his favorite honor roll student took his parking spot located right by the main doors just this once. After all, Jennifer had to hurry if she was to copy off the day's announcements on the copy machine before class. "8:15," the clock read as she zoomed into the school office. Perfect timing. Perfect day ahead. Until . . . "JENNIFER," Mr. Baker yelled as he filled out a parking ticket and detention slip. Guess he wasn't so keen on the idea of her parking in his spot after all.

1._____   2. _____   3. _____
4.____Cereal box____   5. _____   6. _____
7._____   8. _____   9. _____
10._____   11. _____   12. _____
13._____   14. _____   15. _____

Modern Printing Techniques

With the introduction of phototypesetting machines in the 1950s, the production of printed text by means of hot-metal typesetting ended its 500 years of use, but the basic principles first perfected by Johannes Gutenberg are still used today in the publishing industry. Match the modern printing techniques on the left with their common uses on the right. The first one has been done for you.

__D__ 1. **Offset Lithography** uses aluminum plates, rubber blanket cylinders, and photopolymers to print full-color text and illustrations in this inexpensive printing process.

_____ 2. **Letterpress Printing** works well when printing on large rolls or continuous sheets of paper that can be cut into pages later.

_____ 3. **Gravure Printing** uses expensive cylinders and an ink transfer system to print thousands of copies for high-volume printing jobs.

_____ 4. **Flexographic Printing** makes it possible to print images on surfaces other than paper.

_____ 5. **Screen Printing** makes use of stencils and film in printing words and images on fabric and other surfaces.

_____ 6. **Ink-Jet Printing** is used for small jobs like the printing of dates and labels of all kinds.

_____ 7. **Office Copiers** are too slow for use with mass productions, but still find many printing uses today.

_____ 8. **Intaglio Printing** creates a raised texture like that found on some letterheads.

A. Newspapers

B. Plastics, foils, and nonporous materials

C. T-shirts, plastics, banners, circuits, and decorative panels

D. Newspapers, color brochures, catalogs, and food product packages

E. Expiration dates on food packages and address labels

F. Office files, school worksheets, back-up documents

G. Mass circulation magazines and catalogs

H. Business stationery, money, bonds, stock certificates

Instruments of Nautical Astronomy

Before the fifteenth century, a compass, a rudimentary map, familiar landmarks, and simple astronomical signs were the tools used by sailors to navigate their way around the waters of the Mediterranean. But when Portugal's Prince Henry the Navigator decided to explore the Atlantic, the need arose for more sophisticated navigational instruments. The inventions and improvements on instruments of nautical astronomy that Prince Henry pioneered with the founding of the first school of navigation in Europe ushered in the Age of Discovery.

Sail a ship far enough into the ocean that the view from one deck looks identical to the view from another, and you will see that determining your position and charting your course is a challenge when waves and sky are all that are in sight. The astrolabe, one of science's most ancient instruments, whose invention has been credited to the first-century A.D.'s Greek astronomer Hipparchus, assisted sailors in finding their latitude by estimating the altitude of a celestial body. Although not very accurate, especially when used in rough waters, it continued to be the principle instrument of navigation until replaced by the sextant in the 1700s. Bartolomeu Dias, Vasco da Gama, Christopher Columbus, Pedro Álvares Cabral, John Cabot, and Ferdinand Magellan all relied on the astrolabe as they forged new maritime trading routes to new worlds.

Today radio and electronic navigational devices, advanced satellite systems that depend on the Doppler effect, and inertial navigational tools that sense the motion of a craft in relation to where it started have replaced most systems of nautical astronomy in guiding ships (and now airplanes and spacecraft as well), but the efforts of Prince Henry the Navigator have not been forgotten. His desire to explore the open sea led to the invention of navigational tools that have taken humankind around the world, into the sky, and beyond the confines of planet Earth.

List present-day careers that rely on an understanding of advanced navigational tools:

_____

_____

Out to Sea

Use a dictionary or encyclopedia to help you define the following marine, air, and space navigational terms in complete sentences.

1. *Gyrocompass:* _____

   _____

2. *Sextant:* _____

   _____

3. *LORAN:* _____

   _____

4. *Doppler Effect:* _____

   _____

5. *Reckoning:* _____

   _____

6. *Chronometer:* _____

   _____

7. *Altimeter:* _____

   _____

8. *Radar:* _____

   _____

9. *Global Positioning System:* _____

   _____

10. *Guidance and Control Systems:* _____

    _____

11. *Log:* _____

    _____

12. *Mercator Projection:* _____

    _____

Your Ship Has Come In

In addition to promoting advancements in navigational tools, Henry the Navigator oversaw improvements in shipbuilding techniques, which also contributed to the successful adventures of explorers during the Age of Discovery. Imagine you are a sailor during the fifteenth century working aboard a ship sent out from Portugal to open a sea route of trade to India. Complete the story starter below and draw a picture of your ship on the back of this page. Be certain you research the design of fifteenth-century ships in an encyclopedia before attempting your illustration.

We had been afloat in a calm sea of blue, plotting our course easily by the highly visible sun by day and bright stars by night for 21 happy days when the captain reminded us that no trip at sea is without its thunderstorm, navigational mistake, food shortage, or sailor conflict. We all took his warning seriously, but none of us could have imagined the magnitude of the calamities that were to follow.

_____

_____

_____

_____

_____

_____

_____

_____

_____

_____

_____

_____

_____

_____

_____

The Steam Engine

In 1690 the French physicist, Denis Papin, developed a piston-operated water pump, and for the first time in history, power was produced without the use of human or animal muscle, wind gusts or flowing water; and the world would never be the same. Thomas Savery's Miner's Friend of 1698 (a device which used a vacuum to draw water from a flooded mine), Thomas Newcomen's 1705 atmospheric engine, and James Watt's series of inventions that made the steam engine practical for general use ushered in a new era of steam-powered factories and mills, waterworks and pumps, and passenger and cargo trains and ships. The Industrial Revolution had begun and the social and economic structures of the world were about to undergo irreversible transformations.

The widespread use of the steam engine generated a chain of events that included all of these dramatic changes:

- The agriculturally based economies of Europe and the United States became product-based economies as new steam-powered inventions in the steel and cotton industries dramatically reduced the time required to produce goods.

- Work, which was previously done by families on farms and within homes, was now completed in factories and within firms and public enterprises.

- Manufactured products such as picture frames and dress shirts replaced the production of primary products such as wood and cloth that consumers once bought.

- Large cities sprang up throughout Europe and the United States as workers moved from farms to factories.

- The principles of assembly line production created once unheard of routine, specialized jobs.

- World trade evolved with steam-powered transportation moving the newly manufactured products.

- Transportation infrastructures including canals, roads, and railroads were laid all over the United States and Europe to accommodate product distribution.

- New class distinctions arose encompassing the capitalists who owned the factories and machinery and the workers who operated the machines.

Are there any countries in today's world that have not yet felt the effects of the Industrial Revolution that began in England at the end of the eighteenth century with the widespread use of the steam engine? _____

Cause and Effect

The invention of the steam engine spawned the invention of numerous new labor-saving machines and manufactured products during the Industrial Revolution of the late eighteenth through the late nineteenth centuries. How much do you know about this innovative era in European and American history? See if you can match the inventions with their inventors below as you refresh your memory on the details of this time period. If you get stuck, use an encyclopedia to help you. The first one has been done for you.

__D__ 1. Cyrus McCormick

_____ 2. Benjamin Franklin

_____ 3. James Watt

_____ 4. Richard Trevithick

_____ 5. Guglielmo Marconi

_____ 6. Eli Whitney

_____ 7. Edmund Cartwright

_____ 8. Michael Faraday

_____ 9. Alexander Graham Bell

_____ 10. Samuel Morse

_____ 11. Thomas Edison

_____ 12. Karl Benz

A. Power Loom, 1785

B. Steam-Powered Passenger Automobile, 1801, and Railroad Locomotive, 1804

C. Cotton Gin, 1793

D. Reaping Machine, 1831

E. Double-Acting Steam Engine, 1782

F. Electric Motor, 1821

G. Bifocal Eyeglasses, 1784

H. Telegraph, 1837

I. Electric Light Bulb, 1879

J. Telephone, 1876

K. Gas Engine Automobile, 1885

L. Radio, 1895

All Aboard!

Steam-powered boats and locomotives played an important part in the transport of American passengers and products in the late 1700s and throughout the 1800s. Circle your choice of answers to the true-false questions below by referring to the Steam Transportation Time Line that follows.

Steam Transportation Time Line

1685	Denis Papin suggests that steam could be used to power a boat.
1783	Steam is used to power a boat for the first time.
1790	John Fitch establishes the world's first steamboat passenger service line between Philadelphia and Trenton.
1804	The first practical locomotive is constructed in England by Richard Trevithick.
1815	The United States grants John Stevens, the father of American railroads, the nation's first railroad charter, and the construction of railroads begins.
1815	Steamboats become popular means of transportation along the Mississippi River.
1819	The *Savannah* becomes the first steamboat to cross the Atlantic.
1829	Locomotives are first used for the transport of goods and passengers.
1830	The first United States' locomotive is built.
1840	Steamboats are used regularly to transport goods and passengers across the Atlantic.
1848	All Atlantic seaboard states are connected by rail.
1869	The Union Pacific and Central Pacific railways meet in Omaha, Nebraska, completing the coast-to-coast connection of railroads.
1870	The *Robert E. Lee* beats the *Natchez* in a famous steamboat race that takes the boats from New Orleans to St. Louis in fewer than four days.
1940	Diesel-electric locomotives replace steam engines in the United States.

T F 1. Thirteen years passed between the invention of the first practical locomotive and the first use of trains for the transport of passengers and goods.

T F 2. John Stevens is considered the father of American railroads.

T F 3. The United States was connected coast to coast by railroads by 1829.

T F 4. Denis Papin suggested steam could be used to power a boat nearly 100 years before the first steamboat was constructed.

T F 5. Steamboats were a popular form of transportation along the Missouri River beginning in 1815.

T F 6. Steam locomotives transported goods and passengers in the United States for fewer than 100 years.

T F 7. Trains built in Europe were run on tracks in the United States before this nation built its own locomotives.

The Automobile

A study of the earliest attempts at the construction of self-propelled vehicles would not lead one to believe that the automobile would ever change the world. Christiaan Huygens designed a gunpowder-fueled internal combustion engine in 1678, but it was never built. Isaac Newton created a steam-pressure-propelled machine three years later, but it had no further use than that of a toy. Nicolas Joseph Cugnot constructed a three-wheeled vehicle as early as 1770, but it was used only to transport artillery. Working models of steam-powered wagons were constructed in the late 1770s, and Richard Trevithick introduced the first passenger automobile in 1801. Even when steam coaches were finally put to regular use for the transportation in England some 60 years later, restrictive legislation forced them off the roads and discouraged their further development.

Finally some 200 years after Huygens' first dreams of an internal combustion engine and the introduction of Newton's self-propelled machine, Nikolaus August Otto built an efficient four-cycle gas engine in 1876 and the automobile industry was truly born. In 1893 Henry Ford produced his first experimental model, and by 1911, more than 600,000 steam-, gas-, and electricity-powered automobiles were being driven in the United States alone. The conveyor belt and assembly line production techniques were introduced to car-producing factories in 1913. These two innovations and the Automobile Board of Trade, which prompted members to share patent rights, furthered the creation of new and improved cars even more. By 1980 more than 300 million cars and 85 million trucks and buses were operating throughout the world with one third of them being driven on roads in the United States of America.

How many times have you ridden in a vehicle during the past week?_____

Arms of the Automotive Industry

Automobiles have changed the world not only because they provide us with passenger and product transportation, but also because the automotive industry reaches into so many other related areas of the economy. In the United States, one in every six employees works at a job directly or indirectly related to the automobile industry. Match the jobs from the box with the arm of the industry they fall under. The first one has been done for you.

Automotive Insurance Employees	Automotive Factory Employees
Highway Patrol Officers	Road Construction and Maintenance Employees
Infrastructure Engineers	Automobile Engineers and Designers
Computer Engineers	New and Used Car Dealers
Race Car Drivers	Bus and Taxi Drivers
Car Wash Employees	Oil Refinery Employees
DMV Employees	Mechanics and Body Shop Employees
Driving School Instructors	Advertisement Agency Employees
Farmers and Ranchers	Rural Postal Carriers
Truck Drivers	Traffic and Road Condition Reporters
Meteorologists	Gas Station Attendants
Emissions Controls Employees	Lobbyists, Congresspeople, and Auto Law Makers
Paramedics	Car Importers and Exporters
Auto Rental Agency Employees	Steel, Plastic, Glass, and Rubber Factory Employees

Vehicle and Safety Regulations

Automotive Insurance Employees

_____

_____

_____

_____

_____

_____

Auto Design and Construction

_____

_____

_____

Road Maintenance

_____

_____

Auto Repairs and Maintenance

_____

_____

_____

Transportation of Products and People

_____

_____

Auto Rentals and Sales

_____

_____

_____

Other Jobs That Use Vehicles

_____

_____

_____

A Safe Ride

In 1965 Ralph Nader published a book entitled *Unsafe at Any Speed*; it suggested that the poor design of American cars contributed to deaths and injuries resulting from automobile accidents. Since then, laws have been passed, regulatory commissions established, and automobile designs improved in an effort to make automotive transportation as safe as possible. Draw and label the following safety features on the car below: *headlights, brake lights, turn signals, safety belts, airbags, windshield wipers, anti-lock brakes, padded instrument panels, reinforcement bars on doors, front and rear bumpers, side-mounted reflectors,* and *emergency flashers.*

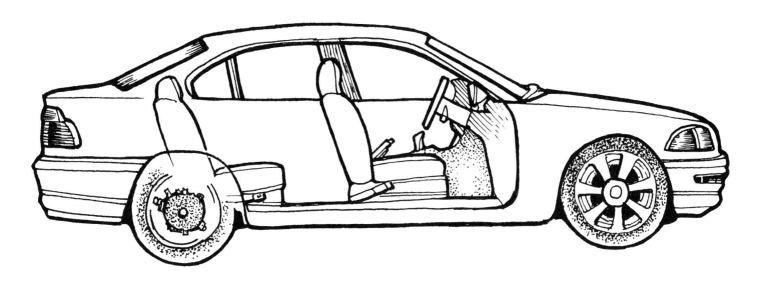

Plastics

In 1860 a company that manufactured billiard balls in the United States offered a $10,000 prize to anyone who could invent an inexpensive substitute for ivory. John Wesley Hyatt did not win the prize with his Celluloid made of cellulose nitrate, camphor, and alcohol, but he did patent a product that was molded into everything from dental plates to photographic film. Totally synthetic plastics followed soon after Hyatt's Celluloid hit the market. In 1920 chemists everywhere began to investigate the claim of Hermann Staudinger that plastics were polymers, or giant molecules. With this research, numerous new plastic product variations were developed such as vinyl and rayon. A shortage of raw materials during World War II prompted the further development of plastics, and the quick pace of advances in the industry carried over into the postwar years.

Today plastic is an indispensable part of industrialized civilizations. Since it is a great barrier against oxygen and water, plastic is most widely used in packaging, but it also creates pipes, insulation, roofing, moldings, hardware products, automotive components, electronic devices, appliances, combs, buttons, brushes, tools, kitchenware items, and more.

Although all are long chains of carbon atoms that can be molded into desired shapes, different types of plastics find different uses. Polyethylene, Plexiglas, Teflon, PVC, nylon, synthetic rubber, Styrofoam, polyesters, and phenol-formaldehydes are just some of the plastics that find commercial uses today. Plastics replace metal, wood, ceramics, glass, and cloth materials because of reduced weight and cost and wider flexibility, but have one major drawback. Plastics are not biodegradable. If not recycled, today's useful plastics become tomorrow's useless refuse.

List here the plastic products that have been a part of your day so far: _____

_____

Do you recycle plastic? _____

A World of Plastic

Read about plastics in an encyclopedia or on the Internet and then match the specific types of plastic listed in the left-hand column with their commercial uses listed in the right-hand column. The first one has been done for you.

Plastics

___F___ 1. Epoxies

_____ 2. Celluloid

_____ 3. Phenol-formaldehyde

_____ 4. Polyethylene

_____ 5. Plexiglas

_____ 6. Teflon

_____ 7. Polyvinyl Chloride (PVC)

_____ 8. Nylons

_____ 9. Polycarbonates

_____ 10. Sulfone

_____ 11. Polyesters

_____ 12. Styrofoam

Uses

A. Bottle caps, wall switches, packaging

B. Eyeglasses, camera lenses, aircraft windows, automotive taillights

C. Combs, brushes, buttons

D. Pipes, hoses, shower curtains

E. Smoke detectors

F. Adhesives, reinforced plastics, surface finishes

G. Textiles, stockings, aerosol valves, bearings, rollers

H. Drinking cups, floatation devices, insulation

I. Bottles, pipes, building materials

J. Glazing, power-tool encasements

K. Textiles, fiberglass boats, fishing rods

L. Cookware, electric circuits

Disposing of the Evidence

How are plastics and other solid wastes disposed of as our nation's landfills overflow and emit toxic gases? Read about the types of waste products and methods of disposal recorded below and then devise a plan for the disposal of your town's waste by addressing the questions on the next page.

Types of Waste

Decomposable Food Waste

Noncombustible Waste (plastic, metal, glass)

Construction and Demolition Debris

Dead Animals

Industrial Wastes (chemicals, paints)

Agricultural Waste

Combustible Waste (cloth, paper, wood)

Ashes

Trees, Grasses, Leaves, etc.

Sewage

Mining Waste

Disposal Methods

Landfill Usage—The cheapest form of disposal, waste is spread into thin layers and covered with alternating layers of soil. Many landfills today are full and closing.

Incinerators—About 70% of solid waste is combustible. Although it causes air pollution and results in ashes that still need to be disposed of, burning waste reduces its volume by about 90%.

Composting—Agricultural and other organic waste can be decomposed into a valuable source of soil nutrients to fertilize crops and potted plants.

Energy Recovery—Garbage can actually be used to produce energy in several different ways. The heat from burning garbage can produce steam for heating buildings, clean-combustion garbage can produce gases to run turbines and generate electricity, and decomposed wastes can produce oil or gas fuels.

Recycling—Paper, glass, metals, and plastics can all be recycled for reuse.

As your city's waste disposal system president, you are commissioned to create a new plan for the disposal of waste in your city now that your local landfill has closed. How will your city dispose of its waste, and how will you get residents to go along with your proposals? Address the following questions in a one- to three-page Waste Disposal Proposal to be presented to your city's council members.

1. Which types of waste as listed on the previous page will your city recycle? Will you ask taxpayers to provide the monies for the construction of recycling plants, or will you ship garbage to existing plants? If garbage will be shipped, how will the shipping be paid for? Will you mandate that plastic, paper, metal, and glass be separated by residents and business owners, or will you hire workers to separate items in a recycling plant?

2. Which methods of disposal will you implement for getting rid of waste products that are not recyclable, but are biodegradable? Why did you choose the methods you did?

3. How will your city dispose of plastic, metal, glass, and other items that are not biodegradable?

4. How will your city dispose of toxic wastes such as paints, chemicals, and industrial waste products?

5. How will you ensure that water resources are not polluted either by waste directly or by your methods of disposing of waste?

6. Will you encourage your city's residents to generate less waste? If so, how will you convince them of the need to use fewer disposable products?

29

Silicon, Integrated Circuits, and the Microprocessor

After oxygen, silicon is the most abundant element on the earth. It constitutes over 25% of the earth's crust and is a part of nearly 40% of all minerals on the planet. Silicon is even found in the sun, other stars, and some meteorites. Yet because it does not occur naturally in its free state, it was not discovered until 1811 when Joseph Gay-Lussac and Baron Louis Thenard prepared an impure silicon mixture; and it was not purified for use until 1824 by Swedish chemist Baron Jöns Jakob Berzelius.

Today silicon is used in the manufacturing of concrete, brick, glass, porcelain, glazes, and cement. It is used in alloy with copper, brass, bronze, and steelmaking. Silica gel is used as a drying and decolorizing agent. Sodium silica preserves eggs; glues the sides of boxes together; binds artificial gemstones, soaps, and cleansers; and acts as an abrasive and a fireproofing agent. Silicone (a silicon-containing compound) is used in the hydraulic systems of airplanes, as an insulator and a waterproofing agent, in construction, and in prosthetic devices.

Yet the most life-altering use of silicon takes place in the world of electronics. Because it acts as a semi-conductor, silicon is effectively used as the wafer on which the integrated circuits of computers, calculators, and digital watches are etched. Thanks to scientific and technological advancements in etching, lithography, film deposition, and oxidation since the first integrated circuit was developed in 1959, a single silicon wafer can now contain the complex circuits of a computer's microprocessor, or central processing unit. A single silicon chip measuring less than a half an inch with an etched surface as thin as one-tenth the thickness of a human hair can now contain the hundreds of complex circuit patterns that operate the sophisticated machines we have come to rely on every day of our lives.

How would life change if all computers were turned off forever?_____

Silicon City

Use a dictionary or encyclopedia to help you define the following words from the world of electronics in complete sentences.

1. *Microprocessor* _____

_____

2. *Central Processing Unit* _____

_____

3. *Integrated Circuits* _____

_____

4. *RAM* _____

_____

5. *Microcontroller* _____

_____

6. *Semiconductor* _____

_____

7. *Transistor* _____

_____

8. *Clean Rooms* _____

_____

9. *Buses* _____

_____

10. *Microcomputers* _____

_____

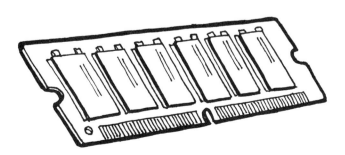

Six-Million-Dollar Man

Many years ago, a television show was based on a character who had numerous artificial body parts that made him stronger than an average man. Thanks to the invention of silicone, a silicon-containing compound developed during World War II, the use of artificial body parts has become very much a reality—although the synthetic prosthetic devices do not make their wearers any stronger. Listed in the box are several silicone medical devices. Label the body below the box with each device to give you an idea of just how widespread the use of silicone has become in the medical world.

Silicone Medical Devices

Artificial Heart Valves	Artificial Vessels in the Eye	Artificial Skin
Artificial Lung	Ear Frame	Pacemaker
Toe Joint	Artificial Hip	Wrist Joint
Finger Joint	Voice Box	Artificial Chin

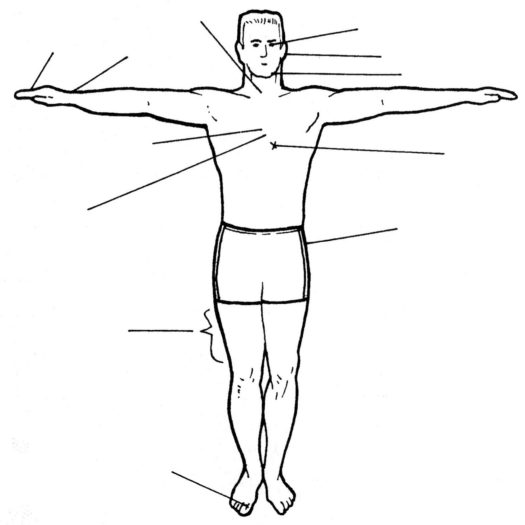

Food Preservation Processes

Protecting food against spoilage has been a goal of humankind since the beginning of time. Prehistoric humans stored meat in ice caves and dried fruits for future use. Ancient cultures used salt to cure fish and ham, and sugar to preserve jellies and jams. For centuries, canning, freezing, smoking, salting, pickling, and cold storage methods have helped people preserve foods. Yet it was not until the invention of refrigerated railroad cars, the invention of refrigerator semi-trucks, and the growth of cities making a complex food distribution system necessary that the preservation of food became big business.

Today numerous preservation techniques are used by the food processing industry, which has become one of the biggest businesses in the United States. Canning exposes foods to high temperatures that destroy bacteria. Freeze-drying and otherwise dehydrating foods eliminate water where bacteria can grow. Refrigerating and freezing foods slow down the growth of microorganisms. Pasteurizing liquids destroys harmful bacteria. Salt and sugar bind water in foods so that bacteria cannot multiply. Chemical additives preserve foods as well as restore nutrients lost during processing and improve texture, color, or taste. An experimental method of compressing foods in water-filled steel cylinders under 16 million pounds of pressure per foot is even being used in Japan to preserve color, texture, and nutritional value in foods without the use of heat or chemicals.

In the absence of all food preservation processes, humankind would not have evolved much beyond hunters and gatherers; but even limiting preservation methods slightly would affect our world. Consider the following:

1. Why would agrarian societies have been unable to evolve into industrial ones in the absence of complex food preservation and distribution systems? _____

   _____

2. How would life be different if the electric refrigerator were never invented? _____

   _____

3. How would the distribution of food change if canning and freezing could not be accomplished on a large scale? _____

   _____

To Market, To Market . . .

See whether you can put in proper sequence the following steps a food product takes on its trip from the farm to your "fridge." Step 1 has been labeled for you.

_____ A farmer sells his/her product to a collection point, such as a grain terminal or stockyard.

_____ A processed food product is sent to a warehouse.

_____ A truck transports the food product to retailers in a given region.

___1___ A plant or animal food product is grown.

_____ A processing company selects raw materials from a stockyard or grain terminal.

_____ A processing company preserves and packages a food product.

Shiny Apples, Crunchy Flakes

Match the food additives on the left with their uses on the right. The first one has been done for you.

___C___ 1. Iron, minerals, vitamins

_____ 2. Lecithin

_____ 3. Antioxidants

_____ 4. Pectin and gelatin

_____ 5. Saccharin

_____ 6. Benzoates and sorbates

_____ 7. Nitrites

_____ 8. Essential oils and resins

_____ 9. Ascorbic acid

_____ 10. Dyes and colors

A. Thicken jellies, jams, ice creams, and marshmallows

B. Slow the growth of yeast, bacteria, and molds

C. Replace nutrients lost in processing

D. Prevent discoloring of canned fruits

E. Sweeten foods

F. Emulsify salad dressings and chocolate

G. Improve appearance of foods

H. Add flavor and fragrance to foods

I. Preserve oils and prevent discoloring in smoked meats

J. Preserve meats

Raking the Muck

In 1906 Upton Sinclair wrote a novel called *The Jungle* that exposed the unsanitary conditions in a Chicago meat-packaging industry. His work led to the passage of the Pure Food and Drug Act that regulates food processing practices even today. Other "muckrakers" of the early twentieth century focused on abuses in business and politics. Research the people below to determine which reform each influenced. The first one has been done for you.

Teddy Roosevelt	Upton Sinclair	Samuel McClure
Lincoln Steffens	Edwin Markham	Harvey Washington Wiley
Ida M. Tarbell	Ray Stannard Baker	Thomas Lawson

___Edwin Markham___ 1. This author of the famous poem "The Man and the Hoe" based on a Millet painting dedicated his life to causes of social justice including a crusade against child labor.

_____ 2. This founder of *McClure's* magazine promoted reforms of all kinds in the United States during the early twentieth century by publishing articles that exposed corruption in politics and business.

_____ 3. This man prompted an investigation into stock market manipulation with the publishing of his 1905 book *Frenzied Finance*.

_____ 4. This man coined the term *muckraker* to denigrate journalists who wrote sensational accounts of political and business corruption, but as president of the United States from 1901-1909, he oversaw numerous social reforms initiated by the writers.

_____ 5. One of the founders of the muckraking movement, this man wrote widely read articles about corruption in the worlds of business and city government, as well as an autobiography that describes the entire muckraking movement.

_____ 6. This woman's exposure of the corruption in the Standard Oil Company led to the company's eventual prosecution.

_____ 7. A chemist with the U.S. Department of Agriculture until 1912, this man's campaign against impure food handling and preservation led to the passage of the first U.S. food and drug law in 1906.

_____ 8. This man's book about the meat-packing industry entitled *The Jungle* also influenced the passage of food and drug laws.

_____ 9. This author of *Following the Color Line* exposed practices of racial discrimination in early twentieth-century America.

IDEAS THAT CHANGED THE WORLD

The Wheel

When you think of wheels, you probably envision cars and trucks and motorcycles, or maybe even bicycles and wheelbarrows. However, the concept of mechanically controlling the direction and/or magnitude of force has been applied to virtually all areas of life since the invention of the wheel around the year 3500 B.C. A solid wooden disk was first used by the Mesopotamians as a potter's wheel that assisted in the formation of clay into bowls and vessels. Then, it was mounted on axles to drive carts. This solid wooden disk of old—and the idea behind it—has since been applied to the wheel and axle, gears, pulleys, and any number of simple and complex technologies. Indeed, many historians argue that the wheel is the most important invention of all time.

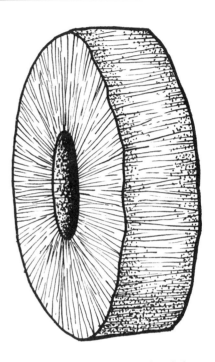

The effectiveness of a wheel in changing the strength or direction of an **applied force** depends on how the wheel is used. When a rope is looped around a grooved wheel to create a **pulley**, the direction of force is changed so that by pulling down on a rope a person can lift an object up. Adding more pulleys to create a movable pulley system not only changes the direction of the force, but also its **magnitude** depending on the number of rope segments created. When a large wheel and a small wheel share the same center to create **wheel and axle**, a small force applied to the large wheel exerts a large force on the small wheel. So, for example, if the large wheel is ten times the size of the small wheel, a person turning a wheel and axle can lift a load ten times the size of the force he/she exerts on the crank or handle. When a wheel is toothed and connected to other toothed wheels in an arrangement of **gears**, rotating motion can be transferred from one part of a machine to another. In each case, a **mechanical advantage** (the ratio of **output force** to **input force**) is gained. Recognizing the mechanical advantage of the wheel has saved humanity an infinite amount of energy throughout time.

List the "hidden" wheels you have encountered today. _____

_____

As the Wheel Turns

Define each of the words that appears in bold type on the previous page in a complete sentence.

1. *Applied Force* _____

_____

2. *Pulley* _____

_____

3. *Magnitude* _____

_____

4. *Wheel and Axle* _____

_____

5. *Gears* _____

_____

6. *Mechanical Advantage* _____

_____

7. *Output Force* _____

_____

8. *Input Force* _____

_____

Simple Machines

A machine is something used to change the direction or strength of an applied force. The four simple machines are the wheel and axle, the pulley, the lever, and the inclined plane. Although the wedge and the screw are often considered simple machines, they are actually adaptations of the inclined plane. Complex machines are nothing more than simple machines used in combination. Match the following examples of the use of simple tools with the type of tool each exemplifies. The first one has been done for you.

Wheel and Axle—Two wheels—one small and one large—that share the same center so that the effect of a force exerted on the large wheel is magnified in the small wheel
Pulley—A rope looped around a grooved wheel used to change the direction of an applied force
Lever—A bar that moves around a fixed point to multiply an applied force
Inclined Plane—A surface inclined to the horizon and used to decrease the effort required to lift or lower an object (including the screw and the wedge)

___Lever___ 1. A farmer transports compost to a compost pile in a *wheelbarrow*.

_____ 2. A mother turns a *faucet handle* to draw a bath for her child.

_____ 3. A grocery clerk maneuvers a grocery cart down a *ramp*.

_____ 4. An elementary school student uses *scissors* to cut paper.

_____ 5. A bucket of water is pulled out of a well with a *rope looped over a wheel*.

_____ 6. A boy and a girl play on a *see-saw* in the park.

_____ 7. A carpenter uses a *screwdriver* to drive a screw into wood.

_____ 8. A chef turns the hand *crank* of a mechanical ice-cream maker.

_____ 9. A lumberman uses an *axe* to chop wood.

_____ 10. *Gears* are used in the operation of a wristwatch.

_____ 11. A *block and tackle* hoists heavy objects.

The Phonetic Alphabet

The alphabet song is probably one of the first recitations you learned upon entering grade school way back at the age of five. In no time, you were reading and writing English. By now you likely take for granted the fact that arbitrary symbols (letters of the alphabet) can represent different sounds and be put together to form words. Communication through writing, however, has not always been so readily accomplished. The idea that written symbols could represent objects and concepts has been around since cave dwellers first began drawing pictures on walls some 30,000 years ago. But the development of an abstract alphabet based on individual sounds did not appear until around 1600 B.C.

Before the development of alphabets, written languages were not based on the sounds of words, but upon the meaning of words. So the cuneiform of the Babylonians and the hieroglyphics of the ancient Egyptians used specific pictures to symbolize objects and ideas. This concrete system of writing required readers and writers to learn as many as 600 signs and made the expression of abstract ideas slow and laborious. So when the people of the eastern Mediterranean developed the world's first alphabet some 3,000 years ago, the concept caught on like wildfire. Soon the Hebrews, Greeks, and Arabs were all devising their own alphabets which allowed writers to convey simple or complex ideas quickly, based on word sounds rather than word meanings. Today nearly all written languages are based on a phonetic alphabet—many of them using the Greek letter system we use to represent sounds in their own tongues. Even the Japanese and Korean languages use symbols to stand for spoken syllables, and the Chinese include some phonetic elements in their otherwise pictorial system of writing.

Representing every object or concept you wished to communicate in picture form would certainly slow down the process of writing. Do you think it would also slow down your thinking processes and make it more difficult to think about abstract ideas that are not easily translatable into pictures? Why or why not? _____

_____

_____

Locate the definitions of *abstract* and *concrete* in a dictionary. Why would it be difficult to represent abstract ideas in hieroglyphics or cuneiform? _____

_____

CU

When ancient Egyptians and Babylonians wished to express an abstract idea in writing, they wrote a sign beside a picture to indicate to the reader that the drawing should be interpreted to mean a word that sounded like the picture but held a different meaning (homophones). An example of this rebus-style writing might be the drawing of a sun accompanied by a special symbol indicating the picture was to stand for the word "son."

Read the following rebus by interpreting the drawings included either literally or as homophones for the word each picture represents. Write the word below each picture.

One day, gave my small a and a hug

and I caught an to Paris for a business meeting. My gave me

his biggest ⌣ and as I flew into the night. Paris was hot and I began to

 myself with a 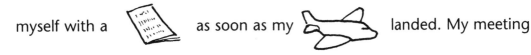 as soon as my 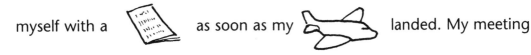 landed. My meeting

was long and began to miss my right off the  .

As soon as had a chance, gave my a on

the . He missed me . We decided right then and there that the

next time took an to a business meeting across the C , my

would come along!

ABCs

The first known alphabet called the North Semitic Alphabet evolved from cuneiform and hieroglyphic symbols. Because pictures were difficult to draw into clay or wax, stylized signs replaced representational pictures. Soon the stylized signs no longer even resembled the original pictures, and they began to symbolize syllables rather than whole words. Eventually, signs represented individual sounds rather than complete syllables, and a true phonetic alphabet was born. Match the letters from the Roman alphabet, which is the basis of written language for English speakers as well as for most other Indo-European languages, with their origin as described below. The first one has been done for you.

| A | B | E | H | I | M | N | P | S | T |

__A__ 1. Originating from the ancient Egyptian symbol for an eagle, the Phoenicians renamed this letter *aleph* meaning "ox" due to its resemblance to an ox's head and horns.

_____ 2. This most frequently used letter in the English language was adopted from the Greek letter *epsilon*.

_____ 3. This letter, which is normally silent in the Roman language and often silent in English when it proceeds a vowel, originated from the Semitic letter *cheth*.

_____ 4. This letter was derived from the Greek letter *pi*.

_____ 5. This letter, *beta* in Greek, is combined with the Greek letter *alpha* to form the word "alphabet."

_____ 6. This letter, which was derived from the Greek letter *mu*, originated with the Egyptian hieroglyph for "owl."

_____ 7. In the Phoenician alphabet, this letter was used to mark ownership.

_____ 8. This letter was derived from the Egyptian hieroglyph symbolizing "hand."

_____ 9. This letter taken from the Egyptian hieroglyph for waterline claimed the Phoenician name, *nun*, or "fish."

_____10. This letter was derived from the Greek letter *sigma*.

The Concept of Free Trade

From the 1500s through the 1800s, the foreign exchange of consumer goods throughout Europe was regulated by tariffs and governmental restrictions based on the economic principle of mercantilism, which suggests that a country must maintain a surplus of exports over imports. In the early nineteenth century, Adam Smith suggested it would be more practical to allow countries with a surplus of natural resources necessary for the production of certain goods to supply those goods to other countries while the other countries, in turn, traded the goods they were best at producing. David Ricardo and John Stuart Mills elaborated on Smith's ideas, and together their theories formed the basis for the concept of free trade.

Free trade refers to the foreign exchange of goods among countries without the restrictions of tariffs and quotas. Although completely unrestricted trade has seldom been practiced by any nation, most modern countries favor free trade and participate in trade agreements that discourage restrictive trading policies. The United States entered into agreement with 22 other nations in 1945 when the international trade organization called the General Agreement on Tariffs and Trades (GATT) came into being and continued its membership when GATT was taken over by the World Trade Organization in 1995. In 1996 the World Trade Organization boasted a membership of 120 nations. Canada, Mexico, and the United States signed the North American Free Trade Agreement in 1994, and talks have addressed the possibility of expanding the treaty to include several Latin American nations as well. European countries have organized under the umbrellas of the European Free Trade Association, the European Economic Community, and the European Union to promote economic cooperation and unrestricted trade among the nations of that continent. They even expect to establish a common European currency by the end of the twentieth century.

The result of political and economic powers favoring free trade in theory, even if not completely in practice, has been a recent shift in finances toward a global economic system. Today trading, customs, and immigration agreements are lax enough in nations around the globe that goods are produced in one country for companies based in another country. Second, natural resources are imported and exported from one shore to another with few restrictions, and banks and businesses have chains that span the globe. Finally, the financial recessions, inflationary periods, and depressions that affect one nation reverberate around the world.

What are the advantages of free trade and a global economic system? _____
_____

Protectionists contend that high tariffs, stringent quotas, and strict governmental restrictions on trade protect a nation by increasing employment within its borders, avoiding dependence on foreign sources of supplies that might be necessary during times of war, and promoting the development of domestic industries. Are these valid advantages to exercising protected trading? Why or why not? _____
_____

Define the following words found in the reading:

Tariffs: _____

Mercantilism: _____

Surplus: _____

Exports: _____

Imports: _____

Natural Resources: _____

Free Trade: _____

General Agreement on Tariffs and Trades: _____

World Trade Organization: _____

North American Free Trade Agreement: _____

European Union: _____

The European Community

The European Community has arguably moved the farthest on the path toward free trade and international cooperation. Conduct research on the history, organization, and purpose of the European Union and determine which of the following are goals or accomplishments of the organization. Write "yes" beside the statements that describe a European Union goal or accomplishment and "no" beside those statements that do not describe a European Union achievement. The first one has been done for you.

__No__ 1. The European Union aims to eliminate all European national borders and create a single European state.

_____ 2. The European Union hopes to establish a common European currency.

_____ 3. The European Union grants European citizenship to all member nations.

_____ 4. The European Union has declared an official continental religion.

_____ 5. Under the Treaty of the European Union, border controls between member countries were relaxed.

_____ 6. Under the Treaty of European Union, custom and immigration agreements have made it easier for citizens of member nations to work, live, and study in other member nations.

_____ 7. An economic and social council belonging to the European Union allows regional employer and employee groups to have a vote on European Union affairs.

_____ 8. A European Union Court of Justice settles disputes between member governments and European Union institutions.

_____ 9. The European Union holds the goal of eliminating all trade barriers between member states and creating a single market.

_____10. All European Union member states maintain a common tariff on goods imported from other parts of the world.

_____11. European Union member nations adopt common policies on everything from taxes to issues of employment, health, and the environment.

Ideas of the Reformation

Before the sixteenth century, church and state were closely intertwined. The king had his armies, but the pope had moral authority. Although they did not clash openly, they constantly vied for supreme power. Rome, being home of the pope, was the primary center of the political universe. Germany, England, France, the Scandinavian countries, Switzerland, the Netherlands, and Scotland all paid papal taxes and adhered to religious and political laws composed in Rome. The Catholic Church, in fact, had acquired as much as one third of all the land of Europe before its authority began to crumble.

Greed and corruption in the church hierarchy, the translation of the Bible from Latin into languages of common folks, a great schism in the Catholic Church, and the growth of a secular intellectual community contributed to a Protestant revolution. The Reformation began in the year 1517 and led not only to the splintering of Christianity into numerous sects, but also to a whole new socio-economic and political system that would govern the regions of Europe. When Martin Luther posted his 95 theses to the church doors in Wittenberg, Germany, challenging the papal demands for monetary penance, he set off a revolution among peasants and commercial classes who were already weary of abuses of power and financial corruption in the clergy. By the end of the sixteenth century, the church had lost its wealth and power to the middle classes. Numerous European countries had gained political and cultural independence. Religious restrictions on trade had been lifted, secular education had begun to flourish, and democratic governments had begun to spring up everywhere in response to a new respect for individualism. What started as a religious struggle had turned the entire world upside down.

How would life be different today if the pope, or any other religious leader, held more power and wealth than the presidents and monarchs of the world? _____

_____

A Protestant Revolution

What began as a Lutheran Reformation in Germany based on the theses of Martin Luther in 1517, soon spread to all of Europe and took on different forms along the way. Choose one of the following national movements to study further. Write a one- to three-page report on the movement, remembering to indicate how the movement was connected to the Reformation as a whole and how the movement affected developments that led to today's world.

Pre-Reformation Warning Signs
Read about John Wycliffe, John Huss, the Renaissance, and the Great Schism as you learn about the backdrop of the Reformation.

The Reformation in Germany
Study Martin Luther, the Diet of Worms, the Peasants' War, and the Augsburg Confession as you learn how a suggestion for reform within the Roman Catholic Church led to warfare and a whole new church.

The Reformation in Scandinavia
Write about Johann Bugenhagen, Olaus and Laurentlus Petri, and the peaceful move from Catholicism to Lutheranism that took place in Denmark, Sweden, and Norway soon after Martin Luther posted his theses in the early 1500s.

The Two Leaders of Switzerland's Reformation
Report on the life and work of either Huldreich Zwingli or John Calvin—both influential men in the Reformation movement in Switzerland. Learn how Calvin and other Protestants persecuted and killed Catholics and nonconformist Protestants much as the Inquisition persecuted and killed Catholics in Spain and the Netherlands.

The Reformation in France
Read about Lefevre d'Etaples and the Huguenots as you prepare a report on the bloodshed at the St. Bartholomew's Day Massacre and during the 40 years of civil war in France that emerged from the division that grew between Protestants and Catholics in the mid-1600s.

The Reformation in the Netherlands
Report on the warfare and Inquisitions that attempted to prevent the spread of Protestant doctrines in the Netherlands before the Spanish Netherlands became an independent Protestant nation in 1648.

The Reformation in Spain
Read how the Inquisition, which began well before the Reformation as a means of persecuting and killing "heretics" in Spain, turned its attention to Protestants in the 1500s. It was not fully suppressed until 1834.

The Reformation in Scotland
Learn how the citizens of Scotland furthered their independence from France and England while gaining religious reforms as you read about John Knox and the establishment of Calvinism as the national religion in Scotland in the late 1500s.

The Reformation in England
Report on how Henry VIII formed his own national church when the Catholic Church refused to grant him an annulment, and how King Edward VI introduced even more reforms into the Anglican Church after Henry VIII's death.

The Copernican System

Although the idea that the earth and other planets revolve around the sun seems obvious to most people today, it took centuries to convince the church, the general public, and the greater scientific community that this was the configuration of our solar system. As early as 270 B.C., the Greek astronomer Aristarchus of Sambas suggested that the earth might revolve around the sun, but he was ignored because his theory contradicted the popularly held theories of the esteemed Aristotle. Again in the late 1400s, the great artist and scientist, Leonardo da Vinci,

questioned on paper the idea that the earth was a centrally located, stationary body. His writings, which were penned in mirror image, were not discovered and deciphered until centuries later. Finally in 1543, just before his death, Nicolaus Copernicus published a book entitled *On the Revolution of Heavenly Bodies* that would become the definitive work explaining a heliocentric, or sun-centered, system of planets.

Still, the road to the acceptance of a heliocentric system was a long one. When Galileo published evidence supporting Copernicus' theory, he was condemned by the Roman Catholic Church as a heretic and sentenced to life imprisonment, which convinced him to revise his stated opinion. Philosophers were not willing to let go of the theories of Aristotle; astronomers still supported the A.D. 130 postulations of Ptolemy that placed the earth at the center of the universe. Theologians maintained that a belief in a moving earth was not biblically credible.

As influential as the Copernican system has been on astronomy itself, the eventual acceptance of the system transformed all learning by finally freeing science from traditional philosophy and religion, which restrained it for centuries.

What scientific beliefs which we hold true today do you predict will be proven inaccurate in the future? _____

_____

The Men Behind the Movement

Because the Copernican system provided a better explanation for actual celestial observations than did the Ptolemic system before it, it would eventually find acceptance in the scientific community. Copernicus influenced Galileo and Kepler directly, and then Isaac Newton and all astronomers to follow. Match the astronomers below with their achievements. The first one has been done for you.

__D__ 1. This second-century A.D. Alexandrian astronomer believed that the earth stood still in the center of the universe. He was not seriously challenged until Copernicus offered a new view in the sixteenth century.

_____ 2. This advocate of a heliocentric system first wrote his theory in a short pamphlet sometime between 1507 and 1515. The work was not published until the nineteenth century. Even his major work was not published until just before his death in 1543, since this man feared his theory would be unpopular.

_____ 3. This author of the three laws of planetary motion wrote the first textbook based on a Copernican system and added mathematic logic to the theory.

_____ 4. This man's stance against censorship of scientific inquiry by the fields of politics or religion and his refusal to stop professing that the earth revolved around the sun earned him a life imprisonment sentence. However, he served his time in the form of house arrest.

_____ 5. Based on the work of Galileo, Kepler, and Copernicus, this man formulated the law of universal gravitation.

_____ 6. This American astronomer discovered galaxies outside the Milky Way and classified extragalactic systems at the beginning of this century.

_____ 7. This man described the Doppler Effect, which shows that the farther away a galaxy is, the faster it moves away from the Milky Way.

A. Christian Johann Doppler

B. Johannes Kepler

C. Nicolaus Copernicus

D. Ptolemy

E. Sir Isaac Newton

F. Edwin Powell Hubble

G. Galileo Galilei

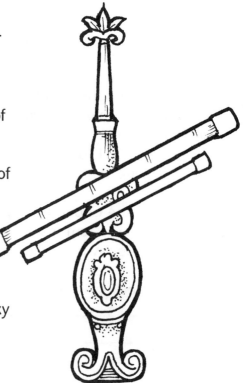

Language of the Stars

Use a dictionary to help you connect the following words from the field of astronomy with their definitions below.

galaxy	quasar	Milky Way	telescope	star
solar system	planet	black hole	comet	asteroid
eclipse	meteorite	orbit	universe	nebula

_____ 1. the name given to the galaxy that includes the earth, our sun, and 100 billion other stars in a radius of about 50,000 light-years

_____ 2. an enormous collection of stars, gas, dust, and planets which contains an average of 100 billion solar masses and ranges in diameter from 1,500 to 300,000 light-years

_____ 3. an interstellar cloud of dust or gas

_____ 4. a celestial body that revolves around the sun and does not emit light

_____ 5. a star-like object that emits light and radio waves

_____ 6. Also known as a minor planet, this type of small celestial body revolves around the sun between Mars and Jupiter.

_____ 7. the term given to the sun and the planets and other bodies that revolve around it

_____ 8. an instrument which uses lenses and mirrors to allow an observer to see distant objects

_____ 9. a ball of frozen dust and gases that develops a tail and halo as it approaches the sun

_____ 10. the term that refers to the complete system of all things that exist

_____ 11. a small mass of matter from outer space that reaches the earth

_____ 12. an area in space with such a strong gravitational field that it holds in everything including light

_____ 13. a mass of hot gases held together by its own gravity

_____ 14. the travel path of a celestial body around another celestial body

_____ 15. the obscuring of one celestial body by another

A Standard System of Musical Notation

Music is a universal art form that has played an important role in human cultures throughout the ages. Instruments have been discovered that date back 30,000 years. Ceremonial music is believed to predate human speech. The rhythms, tones, melodies, and harmonies that become songs are thought to express timeless truths and emotions that connect us with our contemporaries worldwide as well as ancestors in prehistory.

Today music is performed and recorded for many reasons. It is piped in as an auditory background to movies and plays and is associated with dance and poetry (song lyrics). Music is also used as a symbol of group identity among ethic and cultural groups as well as within specific generations. In addition music is put into service as a component of religious and secular rituals and ceremonies. What enables music to fill so many roles? The development of a system of notation based on a chromatic scale, as represented by the black and white keys found on a piano, revolutionized music. Just as the printing press created a revolution in the world of language, the idea that the patterns of tones that comprise a song could be represented on paper changed the world of music forever.

The inscribing of notes onto a musical staff is a system that took centuries to develop. Phonetic and grammatical symbols written above the words of a medieval chant evolved into "neumes" that were positioned above or below a line to indicate vague melodic patterns. By about A.D. 1200, staff lines were used to note an exact pitch. Fifty years later, symbols were standardized to indicate a note's duration. By the fourteenth century time-signatures were added, and by the mid-fifteenth century the system of musical notation in existence was quite similar to the one used today. Forms and uses of music have flourished ever since.

On a sheet of paper, write a tally mark each time you hear music today either internally (humming a tune in your own head) or externally (on the radio, TV, etc.). Do you think you could make it through an entire day without thinking about or listening to music?

Name That Instrument

There are so many musical instruments in the world that systems of classification have been devised to help group and identify them all. Read the brief definitions of the familiar instrument families below and then see whether you can name the pictured instruments and classify them into a family.

Stringed instruments are usually hollow wooden cases threaded with strings that can be bowed, plucked, or hammered.

Wind instruments that are played either with or without reeds are long tubes in which air vibrates to create varying sounds.

Percussion instruments are played by striking or shaking and comprise the oldest instrumental group.

Keyboard instruments, unique to Western musical traditions, include seven white and five black keys per octave that allow performers to play several notes at once.

Instrument #1

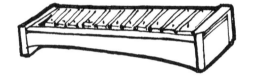

Instrument Name _____
Instrument Family _____

Instrument #2

Instrument Name _____
Instrument Family _____

Instrument #3

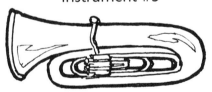

Instrument Name _____
Instrument Family _____

Instrument #4

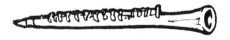

Instrument Name _____
Instrument Family _____

Instrument #5

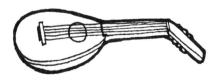

Instrument Name _____
Instrument Family _____

Instrument #6

Instrument Name _____
Instrument Family _____

Making Music

Complete the following crossword puzzle by locating the definition of the musical terms below in a dictionary and following the hints provided.

Across

4. to set a specific key or tone; a baseball term

6. a difference in pitch between two tones

8. a written symbol that stands for a certain tone

10. the succession of individual tones that makes up the main part of a song

11. the main tonality of a musical composition; "The symphony was played in the __ __ __ of C minor."

Down

1. the combining of variously pitched tones in an organized and artistic way

2. a group of tones separated by specific intervals used when music is composed

3. a musical interval of eight diatonic degrees

5. a blending of individual tones into chords

7. a patterned recurring beat or accent

9. a musical sound of a definite pitch

The Concept of Inalienable Rights

Take a few minutes to consider some of the rights you take for granted as a citizen of the United States. If you want to criticize a presidential decision by writing an editorial to be included in your local newspaper, you can do so. If you want to study to become a plumber or a nurse, you do not need governmental approval before enlisting in classes. Should you choose to do so, you could set foot in any public school building, library, restaurant, or movie theater in town regardless of your race, religion, or sex.

People who lived in societies prior to the Reformation of the 1500s or the English, American, and French Revolutions that followed were not so lucky. Because of the widely held belief that all power should be in the hands of a king who was believed to have gained his authority from God, individual citizens could be treated any way a king saw fit. If a person professed a belief that opposed the religion of a king, he could be executed. If a person could not pay his bills or taxes, he could be imprisoned forever. If a king wanted money for a new project, he could raise taxes without warning. If a king did not believe in the equality of slaves or women or noncitizens, they could be legally discriminated against in work and society. And for many, many years, people did not question the treatment they received because a king was believed to answer only to God.

Religious leaders such as Martin Luther and political philosophers including Thomas Jefferson and Jean Jacques Rousseau began to question these long-held ideas of **absolutism** and the **divine right** of kings and popes. They, instead, suggested that human beings are born with certain rights that cannot be infringed upon by the state. These included the freedom of thought, speech, and religion as well as the guarantee of life, liberty, and justice.

As constitutional governments arose out of the revolutions in France, England, and the United States in the 1600s and 1700s, these **inalienable rights** were encoded in legal documents. Today, although minorities and women among other groups continue to struggle for equality in practice, the concept that all human beings are born with the same inalienable rights is a universally accepted philosophy. The Universal Declaration of Human Rights which was adopted by the United Nations General Assembly in 1948 asserts personal, civil, political, economic, social, religious, and cultural freedom for all people of the world.

Name _____

Make a list of rights that you believe all people in the world should share simply because they are human beings: _____

_____

Do children share the same rights as adults? _____

Do animals and plants have "rights"? _____

Locate the bold words from the reading in a dictionary and record their definitions here:

Absolutism: _____

Divine Right: _____

Inalienable Rights: _____

Fighters for Freedom and Equality

Locate the following names in an encyclopedia and then match the philosopher with his capsule biography. The first one has been done for you.

Montesquieu	Thomas Jefferson	James Madison
Jean-Jacques Rousseau	Socrates	Plato
John Locke	John Wilkes	Voltaire
Jeremy Bentham	Thomas Paine	Thomas Hobbes

<u>John Wilkes</u>   1. This British political leader who spent time in prison rather than give up his right to free speech evoked riots among his constituents when the House of Commons invalidated his election three times.

_____ 2. This Frenchman's popular writings helped bring about the French Revolution.

_____ 3. This early Greek disciple of Socrates believed in the freedom of intellectual pursuits.

_____ 4. This English philosopher's attacks on the theory of the divine right of kings greatly influenced the writers of the Declaration of Independence.

_____ 5. This author of the Declaration of Independence was vehemently against "every form of tyranny over the mind of man."

_____ 6. Although he defended the royal prerogative of England's King Charles I, this man's belief that society only exists for the sake of its individual members (individualism) influenced the thinking of John Locke and ultimately encouraged the formation of constitutional governments.

_____ 7. This man who suggested laws should produce "the greatest happiness for the greatest number" was playing violin at the age of 5 and studying law at the age of 12. His fully clothed skeleton is on display at University College in London.

_____ 8. This fourth president of the United States insisted that the Constitution include a Bill of Rights to safeguard religious and intellectual freedoms.

_____ 9. This political theorist wrote *The Social Contract* in 1762, which argued that popular will should govern in place of divine right.

_____ 10. This enemy of Rousseau, who spent time in prison for writing satires about French government, believed in the freedom of thought and encouraged his contemporaries to respect all people.

_____ 11. This teacher of Plato, who wrote no books nor started any official school of thought, influenced Western philosophy as much as any man in history. When he insisted on speaking his own mind in Greece, he was sentenced to death.

_____ 12. This editor of the *Pennsylvania Magazine* condemned slavery, championed inalienable rights, and encouraged the writing of the Declaration of Independence with the anonymous publication of a pamphlet entitled *Common Sense*.

Automation, Interchangeable Parts, and Assembly Line Production

Walk away from a sporting goods store with a tennis racket that was designed by computer and fashioned by a robot. Drive away from a car lot in a vehicle hot off a fully automated assembly line monitored by people who push buttons in a room not even located on the production line floor. Everything from tents to toothpicks is mechanically mass produced today, but that has not always been the case.

Until the late 1800s, consumers bought raw products such as wood and cloth so they could build their own homes or sew their own garments. The few manufactured goods that were produced were one-of-a-kind, expensive, often lifetime purchases built from start to finish by a single craftsperson in his or her own home. A clockmaker would construct clocks one at a time using unique parts in each.

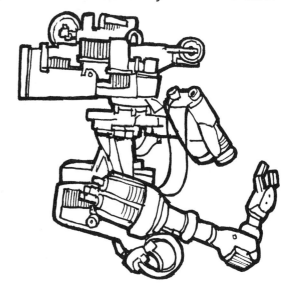

Then came the steam engine, water-powered mills, and specialized machines that gave rise to factories where all of the new devices could be located in one building constructed near an energy source. Within two centuries, the manufacturing process was divided into individual steps, conveyer belts were designed to move "workpieces" through various stages of production, and interchangeable parts replaced one-of-a-kind structures. The modern mass production system was born.

The factory system of production has increased wages, dramatically raised productivity, and made consumer goods affordable and easily available. It has also replaced skilled tradesmen with unskilled laborers, computers, and robots; and it has caused global pollution and indiscriminate destruction of natural resources.

What would be the pros and cons of returning to a world where consumer goods were expensive, one-of-a-kind products constructed by individual craftspersons? _____

_____

_____

Dreamers and Inventors in Manufacturing

Match the following idea men with their contributions to manufacturing by locating their names in your history text or an encyclopedia. The first one has been done for you.

___A___ 1. Samuel Gompers

_____ 2. James Watt

_____ 3. Oliver Evans

_____ 4. Ransom Eli Olds

_____ 5. Sir Richard Arkwright

_____ 6. Adam Smith

_____ 7. Eli Whitney

_____ 8. Henry Ford

A. first leader of the American Federation of Labor and organizer of trade unions established to protect the rights of factory workers and others

B. inventor of a mechanized method of spinning cotton that prompted the mass production of clothing

C. improved the steam engine by adding the flyball governor, which operated on a feedback principle—the key principle in automation

D. popularized the use of interchangeable parts and assembly line production in the automobile industry

E. British economist who first discussed dividing the process of manufacturing into its smallest steps (Division of Labor)

F. founder of the first automobile factory that used assembly line methods of production

G. inventor of the cotton gin and the first to use interchangeable parts in production of manufactured goods (guns)

H. designer of the first automated factory

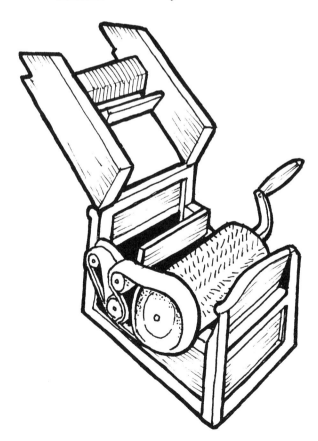

Extraction, Alteration, Microprocessors, and Feedback Loops

Match the manufacturing words from the word box with their definitions below.

Word Box			
Assembly line	Detroit automation	Mechanization	Modern automation
Robots	Mass production	Cybernetics	Transfer machine
Microprocessor	Feedback loop	FMS	Interchangeable parts
Cottage industry	Extraction	Assembly	Computer-aided design
Alteration	CAM	Factories	Artificial intelligence

_____ 1. the use of computers to draft, manipulate, and test model products before the production stage

_____ 2. a built-in system that allows a machine to self-correct according to a predetermined set of standards

_____ 3. the system of mass production that makes use of machines, the assembly line system, and interchangeable parts that first became popular in the automotive industry

_____ 4. a machine that transfers a workpiece from one specialized machine to another and positions it properly so the next step of production can be performed

_____ 5. Short for computer-aided manufacturing, this use of technology allows engineers to determine the most effective set of manufacturing procedures for the production of a specific product with the use of computer modeling before any actual production begins.

_____ 6. This central processing unit of a computer has made possible the use of CAD, CAM, and FMS in modern automation.

_____ 7. This form of production breaks manufacturing down into individual steps that are performed at various stages along a continuously moving line.

_____ 8. This term refers to the manufacturing of a product by means of removing some part of an existing substance. An example of this form of production is the transformation of crude oil into gas.

_____ 9. In this form of manufacturing, an existing substance is transformed into a useful product as with the transformation of trees into lumber.

_____ 10. In this form of production, pieces are put together until an entire product is created, such as with the making of automobiles.

_____ 11. This present-day form of automation goes beyond Detroit automation to include the use of computers and technology at every level of production from scheduling to modeling to the use of self-correcting machines that rely on only a very limited number of humans who do little more than ensure that the technology is in good working order.

_____ 12. a computer's capability of visually recognizing objects on a conveyor belt, understanding human languages, and making decisions based on data much as the human mind does

_____ 13. These machines work faster, make fewer mistakes, and operate easily in conditions hazardous to human beings as they transfer, manipulate, and position workpieces all along an assembly line.

_____ 14. Prior to the Industrial Revolution, most consumer products were one-of-a-kind items created by craftsmen at home. This term defines home-crafted production.

_____ 15. This acronym for Flexible Manufacturing Systems refers to computer control of all operations of a factory from scheduling to production.

_____ 16. In 1798 Eli Whitney experimented with the use of these standardized parts in the production of military muskets. Perfecting the use of standardized parts has been essential to the development of mass production.

_____ 17. term that refers to the manufacturing of consumer goods in large quantities; made possible by the use of assembly line production and interchangeable parts

_____ 18. Although silk was produced in these establishments as early as the Middle Ages, these "production houses" did not become popular until mechanized tools required housing in a single building located close to a power source (originally water).

_____ 19. the science that compares the communications systems of mechanical devices with those in biological organisms

_____ 20. This occurs when machines replace human labor. Unlike automation, this does not refer to self-regulating devices, but rather ones that require human assistance.

IDEAS THAT CHANGED THE WORLD

Psychology: The Study of Behaviors and the Brain

Mention the word *psychology,* and the average person conjures up images of therapists and patients, mental institutions, and Sigmund Freud with his cigar; but the scientific study of behavior and mental processes has contributed a great deal more to the modern world than that which can be seen in the subfield of abnormal psychology. Ever since the seventeenth century human beings have theorized how we think, learn, and sense things. Rene Descartes suggested that the human mind is filled with ideas and personality traits from birth, and John Locke countered that an infant's mind was a blank slate until experience formulated

its contents. Some psychologists stress the importance of genetics while others look at the role of one's upbringing and environment. Physiological psychologists focus on brain structures and the functioning of the nervous system. Behavioral psychologists conduct research on behaviors while social psychologists study how people interact. Industrial psychologists conduct marketing research and occupational training programs as they work with people in their jobs. School counselors guide students to careers and colleges, whereas clinical psychologists work in clinics and hospitals with patients who wish to overcome negative habits or improve the quality of their lives, and psychiatrists work with the mentally ill.

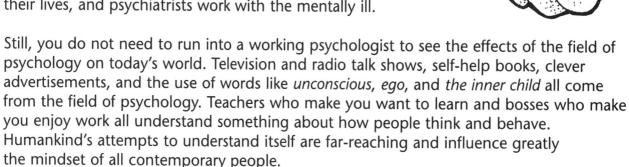

Still, you do not need to run into a working psychologist to see the effects of the field of psychology on today's world. Television and radio talk shows, self-help books, clever advertisements, and the use of words like *unconscious, ego,* and *the inner child* all come from the field of psychology. Teachers who make you want to learn and bosses who make you enjoy work all understand something about how people think and behave. Humankind's attempts to understand itself are far-reaching and influence greatly the mindset of all contemporary people.

When have you used your own understanding of people to accomplish a goal or get your own way?_____

_____

Branches of Psychology

Locate the following branches of psychology in a dictionary or encyclopedia and define the scope of each in complete sentences on your own paper.

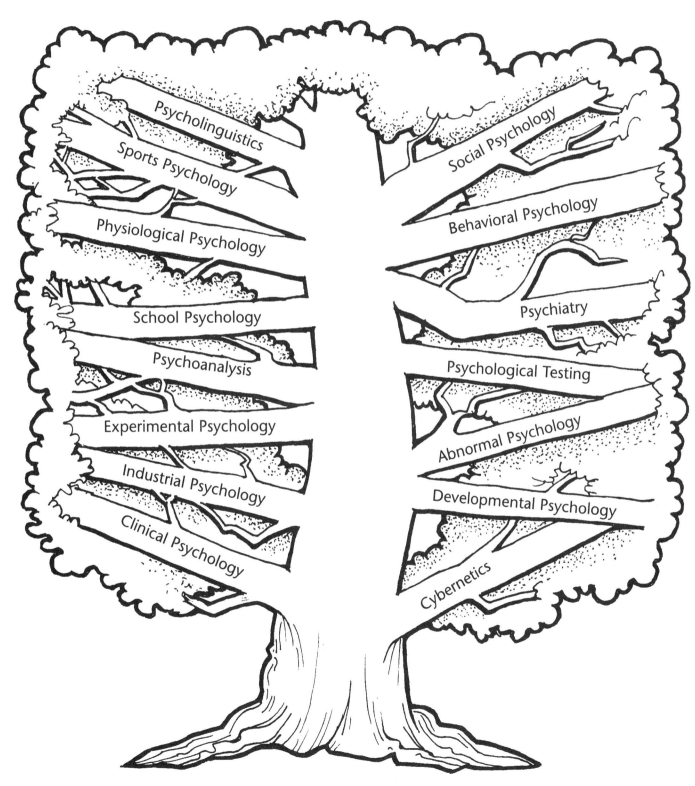

Psycholinguistics

Sports Psychology

Physiological Psychology

School Psychology

Psychoanalysis

Experimental Psychology

Industrial Psychology

Clinical Psychology

Social Psychology

Behavioral Psychology

Psychiatry

Psychological Testing

Abnormal Psychology

Developmental Psychology

Cybernetics

In My Way of Thinking

Determining how the human brain works is not an easy task. Numerous theories attempt to explain all different aspects of how people think, learn, sense, and behave. Read the theories below and then decide whether your own experience confirms them. Give at least one example to support your contention. A sample has been done for you.

1. John Locke suggested that people do not have a "set" intelligence from birth, but learn from experience alone.
   I agree disagree because my sister is much smarter than I am at math and we have
   had all the same teachers. I think she just "gets it" better because her brain is just
   kind of set up to understand math.

2. By extrapolating from experiments with dogs, Pavlov suggested that you will do best on a test if the conditions under which you study match the actual testing conditions closely.
   I agree disagree because _____

   _____

3. Skinner's research suggests that you will find it easier to learn a complete skill if you get rewarded for successful steps along the way.
   I agree disagree because _____

   _____

4. Social psychology suggests that if a friend tells you a movie is great, and you watch it and do not find it so great, you will either think less of your friend, or find reasons to like the movie so that your attitude toward the movie and the friend who recommended it stay in balance.
   I agree disagree because _____

   _____

5. One experiment suggests if you are talking to a friend in the lunchroom and someone across the room mentions your name in a conversation you were not even following, you will hear and focus on your name.
   I agree disagree because _____

   _____

6. Mob psychology suggests that if a large group of people you are a part of begins to do something you would not normally do, you will join in.
   I agree disagree because _____

   _____

7. Some psychologists suggest the brain processes information just like a computer.
   I agree disagree because _____

   _____

The Theory of Relativity

In 1905 Albert Einstein, a patent office employee who never did well in school, published a paper on the special theory of relativity, and virtually no one could comprehend his ideas. In fact, even years later when his work was widely accepted, Sir Arthur Eddington, a British astronomer who helped promote Einstein's theories, was asked by a reporter if it were true that only three people in the world understood the theory of relativity. He reportedly replied, "Who is the third?"

In general, the theory suggests that there is no object in space that can be used as an at-rest frame of reference because nothing in the universe is at rest, and so mass, time, space, and acceleration must all be considered together in any problem. The consequences of his theory are interesting: time proceeds more slowly for a moving object, an event happens at different times to observers moving at different speeds, and an object has a greater mass when moving than when at rest.

Regardless of their incredible nature, Einstein's ideas have been verified experimentally and his theory is one of the most important concepts in physics and astronomy today. The theory of relativity has advanced the understanding of black holes, neutron stars, and the big bang theory. It has revolutionized the way scientists view the elements of space and time, waves and particles, and matter and gravity. After 200 years of basing scientific inquiry on the principles of mechanics developed by the seventeenth century's Isaac Newton, physicists and astronomers now operate under the assumption that we live in a world of curved space-time and that a good theory, as Einstein suggested, is as much the result of a finely tuned intuition as it is the product of experimentation.

Tell a classmate about a time when experience verified something you just "felt" to be true for a long time.

I Wonder . . .

If you dropped a bowling ball and a tennis ball off the roof of your school building at the same instant, which would hit the ground first? If you filled a famous brand soda can with a grocery store brand soda, could your friends tell the difference?

The theory of relativity—and all other advances in science—can be attributed to the curiosity of scientists. Devise a question of your own and conduct an experiment that will answer your concern. Use this activity sheet as a guide to your research.

Answer before conducting your experiment:
What question would you like answered by your experiment? _____

_____

What supplies will you need for your experiment?

_____   _____

_____   _____

_____   _____

How will you conduct your experiment?

Step 1: _____

Step 2: _____

Step 3: _____

Step 4: _____

Step 5: _____

Answer after conducting your experiment:
Describe what you saw during your experiment: _____

_____

_____

What was the result of your experiment? Did it answer your question? If so, what is the answer? If not, why didn't it answer your question? _____

_____

_____

Did you get the results you expected? Why do you think you got the results you did?

_____

_____

_____

Adages and Aphorisms

Albert Einstein was not only a great scientist, but also a great humanitarian who used his fame to speak against war and in favor of the pursuit of truth. Read the following quotations by Albert Einstein on the subjects below and then write a saying of your own, expressing your views on the subject. A sample has been done for you.

On *education:*

Albert Einstein: "Study and, in general, the pursuit of truth and beauty is a sphere of activity in which we are permitted to remain children all of our lives."

Me: _Keeping the curiosity of childhood alive allows you to marvel at the_

wonderment of the world all the days of your life.

On *order in the universe:*

Albert Einstein: "God does not play dice with the world."

Me: _____

_____

On *war and peace:*

Albert Einstein: "Armament is no protection against war but leads to war. Striving for peace and preparing for war are incompatible with each other."

Me: _____

_____

On *the challenges of math:*

Albert Einstein: "Do not worry about your difficulties in mathematics. I can assure you that mine are still greater."

Me: _____

_____

On *the theory of relativity:*

Albert Einstein: "Any physicist who tries can understand it."

Me: _____

_____

On *society:*

Albert Einstein: "Any social organism can become psychically distempered just as any individual can."

Me: _____

_____

Fascism, Nazism, and Totalitarian Regimes

On June 28, 1919, World War I ended with the signing of the Treaty of Versailles. Under the imposed agreement, Germany lost all of its colonies and much of its political and economic clout. The high unemployment and seemingly endless depression that followed precipitated the formation of the National Socialist Party. By 1933 the party had gained enough seats in the German legislature and enough popularity with the German people that President Hindenburg felt compelled to appoint the party's leader, Adolf Hitler, to the position of chancellor of the country. By that same time in Italy, Benito Mussolini had already transformed his country into a totalitarian regime in which all social, economic, and political activities conformed to his whims. Together the fascists governments that ruled Italy and Germany between the two world wars dramatically changed the course of history.

Under totalitarian governments, members of the ruling party become the elite; mass communications are controlled by the state; terroristic secret police monitor civilian behaviors; and the economy is centrally controlled. Trade unions are abolished, opposing political parties are outlawed, and labor and resources are taken from civilians to satisfy the needs of the state. Under Mussolini, Italy enacted anti-Jewish laws, murdered political rivals, invaded Albania, and aided General Franco in the Spanish Civil War and Hitler in his myriad conquests. In Germany, Nazism led to the extensive use of slave labor and the systematic killing of millions of Jews, Poles, Russians, and others. Hitler's invasion of Poland initiated World War II, which became the most destructive conflict in human history and involved more civilians than any war before it.

What factors might lead to the citizens of a nation supporting a political system that advocates violence and terroristic activities—even among its own people—and prohibits so many individual freedoms? _____

_____

Totalitarian Time Line

Although the fascists regimes of Italy and Germany ended with World War II, totalitarian governments continue in some countries of the world today. Match the rulers and countries listed in the boxes with the dates of rule recorded below to create a totalitarian time line. Then choose one of the regimes to research and write about on your own paper.

Rulers

Adolf Hitler   Kim Il Sung
Joseph Stalin   Hafez al-Assad
Mao Tse-Tung   Saddam Hussein
Benito Mussolini

Countries

Iraq   Syria
USSR   China
Germany   Italy
North Korea

1924-1943 Ruler Country
1929-1953 Ruler Country
1933-1945 Ruler Country
1934-1976 Ruler Country
1948-1994 Ruler Country
1970-Present Ruler Country
1979-Present Ruler Country

How Could This Happen?

Millions of human beings died in World War II. Millions more lost their homes and possessions and were forced into slave labor and inhumane living conditions. How such atrocities could happen will probably be beyond human comprehension forever, but we can understand the mindset that allows bad things to happen on a small scale by considering our own lives. Answer the following subjective questions about things that have influenced you to make poor decisions from time to time.

1. Describe a time when you knew someone was getting made fun of or hurt but did not choose to stand up for the person. Why did you decide not to stand up for the victim?

_____
_____
_____
_____

2. Tell about a time you decided to do something you were not comfortable doing because your friends convinced you it was okay to do it. How did you feel afterwards?

_____
_____
_____
_____

3. Tell about a time you made a conscious decision to make fun of someone or otherwise make a person feel bad. What led to your poor decision? How did you feel afterwards?

_____
_____
_____
_____

4. Describe a time when you joined others in name calling, bullying, or gossiping unkindly about another person.

_____
_____
_____
_____

Abstract Art

As scientific and technological advancements have revolutionized the mindsets and lifestyles of twentieth-century people, modern concepts in art have significantly reflected social change. Prior to the French avant-garde paintings of the nineteenth century, art attempted to symbolically or realistically represent images from the real world. Landscapes, scenes from everyday life, and portraits were common subjects for the artist before the invention of the camera diminished the need for realistic representational art. Even metaphorical scenes and stylized drawings represented something from the real world. If a king were drawn unrealistically three times the size of his lowly subjects in a painting, a viewer could still determine that the figures on the canvas represented human beings.

Then came the abstract art of the twentieth century. Abstract art is not intended to represent objects from the real world. For example, a painting titled *The Chair* may look nothing like any piece of furniture at all. Instead, an emphasis on style, lighting, color, and motion may result in a piece of artwork that expresses the artist's subjective impulses and emotions as he contemplated a chair. Because the essence of modern art is to set free the dreams and unconscious will of the artist, what may appear as nothing more than splotches of multicolored paint, senseless stark black lines, or simple geometric figures floating in space may represent the spontaneous expressions of a free thinking artist.

Whether or not abstract paintings appeal to you, the critical acceptance of nonrepresentational art based on the subjective outlooks of individual artists legitimizes free thought in one more area of modern humanity.

Do you prefer viewing art that represents something from the real world, or abstract art that is intentionally nonrepresentational? _____

_____

Making Sense of Modern Art

Even if it all looks the same to you, there are numerous schools in the world of modern art, each sharing specific characteristics and techniques. Match the artists from the box with the style in which they painted. The first one has been done for you.

Salvador Dali	Mark Rothko	Jackson Pollock
Henri Matisse	Andy Warhol	Grandma Moses
Willem de Kooning	Pablo Picasso	Kenneth Noland

__Jackson Pollock__   1. *Gesture Painting* involves working with accident, chance, and spontaneous dripping and pouring of paints to create a uniquely balanced and untraditionally composed painting.

_____   2. *Action Painting* uses broad brush strokes to create the illusion of rhythm and texture.

_____   3. *Surrealism* results in abstract representative images due to its emphasis on the importance of the subconscious mind in the creation of art.

_____   4. *Fauvism* uses rhythm, lines, and brilliant colors to express emotion and movement.

_____   5. *Minimalism* reduces images to simple geometric forms, rhythmic patterns, and single colors.

_____   6. *Primitivism* employs bright colors and simple figures and scenes.

_____   7. *Cubism* represents the many angles of a subject at once, focusing on geometric shapes and bold colors and textures.

_____   8. *Color Field Painting* explores the use of subtle colors to cover an entire canvas.

_____   9. *Op-Art* produces abstract optical illusions.

Expressly Me

Use markers or crayons to express yourself artistically using modern art techniques.

Surrealist Automation: This is the artistic equivalent of a "free writing." Without stopping to reflect on what you are drawing, splash colors and lines that express your present mood, emotions, and thoughts into the box.

Action Painting: Use broad strokes to create the illusion of rhythm and texture.

Cubism: Draw a common object using bright colors and focusing on the object's sharp angles. Include many angles in a single illustration.

Color Field Painting: Color the entire square in light, muted colors.

Primitivism: Use stick-like figures and bright colors to illustrate a common school scene like a classroom or filled football stadium.

The Internet

In 1973 Vinton Cerf developed a network of computers for the U.S. Department of Defense Advanced Research Project Agency so that the agency's computers could communicate with one another. In 1989 Timothy Berners-Lee expanded the concept to develop the World Wide Web. By 1996 the Internet connected more than 25 million computers in over 180 countries. Today government officials, business people, students, and everyday PC owners can all get on-line and unlock what has become the world's largest file cabinet. Surfers of the Net can send e-mail and faxes, communicate with friends and strangers in chat rooms around the world, buy merchandise, and complete extensive research without ever leaving their living rooms. Business executives can buy and sell stock, advertise job openings, complete marketing research, and follow the latest trends in their field on the Internet. Teachers can download complete lesson plans; and students can compile extensive, up-to-date information necessary for report writing. Medical scientists can post current research findings, and doctors can use the ever-changing information to modify their strategies in treating patients. College graduates can post their resumes, amateur philosophers can post their philosophies, and grandmothers can post their entire album of grandchildren's pictures.

The impact of the ever-increasing use of the Internet is only beginning to be seen today. Will e-mail completely replace the postal service? Will on-line banking and business make cash obsolete? Will broadcast television be upstaged by unicast which will send customized programming to interested homes so each family can watch what they want when they want to watch it? Will conflicts over the issue of censorship and the rightful ownership of ideas posted on the Net retard the growth of the Internet industry? Much remains to be seen, but already the simple idea that computers could be networked together has begun to dramatically change our world.

On your own paper, predict an answer to each of the questions posed in the last paragraph of the reading.

Computer Connections

Read about how computers transmit and interpret information and then draw a diagram connecting computer A to Computer B.

1. A computer is connected to a local network called a *gateway* using a computerized address.
2. Gateways are connected to one another using telephone lines, optical fibers, and radio links.
3. Browsers use hypertext transfer protocol (http) to retrieve requested files.
4. Http reads and interprets files on a destination computer.

Computer A

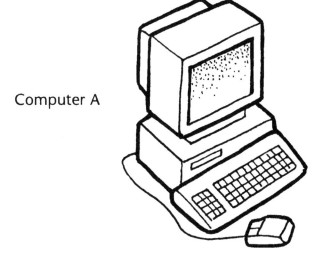

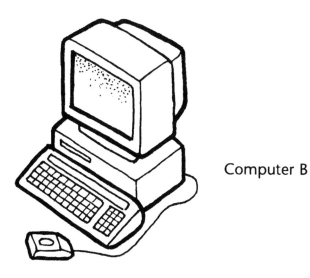

Computer B

Name _____

Internet Access

Government offices, college libraries, members of the business community, and private citizens all make data available on the Internet. Browsers categorize the volumes of information into subject areas so that surfers of the Net can access information about virtually anything. See if you can locate the following information on the Internet. List the web address where you found the information. Since several sites contain information on the same subject, there are several right answers to these exercises. An answer key is provided with one possible solution to each. The first one has been done for you.

At what Internet address might you find . . .

1. . . . the complete text of the United States Constitution?
   www.law.cornell.edu/constitution/constitutionoverview _____

2. . . . the mailing addresses of your state representatives in Washington? _____

3. . . . a map of Thailand? _____

4. . . . today's top news stories? _____

5. . . . chicken recipes? _____

6. . . . the telephone number of a book store near you? _____

7. . . . today's weather conditions in Florida? _____

8. . . . the current price of an airline ticket to London? _____

9. . . . a complete list of books by Roald Dahl? _____

10. . . . reviews of current movies? _____

11. . . . biographical information on Albert Einstein? _____

12. . . . information on four-year, accredited colleges in California? _____

_____

PEOPLE
WHO CHANGED THE WORLD

Ancient Greek Philosophers: Socrates, Plato, and Aristotle

The modern fields of politics, science, education, **philosophy**, law, religion, psychology, **ethics,** and **sociology** all owe homage to the profoundly influential ideas that came out of Athens in the third and fourth centuries B.C. The Greek philosopher, Socrates, who lived 469-399 B.C., invented a method of thinking now referred to as the Socratic method, which places an emphasis on asking questions, answering questions, and asking more questions. In fact, Socrates was so convinced of the virtue of **dialogue** in uncovering truths that he spent much of his adult life debating issues of philosophy with passersby in the marketplace. He never recorded any of his beliefs and never **retracted** his conviction in the freedom of thought even when, in the end, it meant a **condemnation** to death by the Greek government.

We know about Socrates only from the writings of his pupil, Plato. Plato wrote down the ideas of Socrates and **expounded** on them in developing his own theories about the nature of goodness, justice, and truth. His work entitled *The Republic* has influenced law and politics in Western civilization over the centuries, and his theories about reason and **rational** thought form the basis of twentieth-century philosophy. In 387 B.C. Plato founded the Academy of Athens, Europe's first university, and educated yet another influential Western philosopher—Aristotle.

Aristotle was the founder of biology, the father of **literary criticism,** and the first to use logic in an effort to systematically organize all human knowledge. He advised monarchs, taught students, and wrote **treaties,** poems, and letters. He expanded knowledge on logic, **physics**, metaphysics, ethics, and literature. He promoted justice, courage, and the **pursuit** of truth and beauty, and asserted that happiness lies in avoiding extremes.

Use a dictionary to define all of the words in bold in this reading on your own paper.

Greek Influence

Learn just how influential ancient Greek philosophers have been to the development of politics, philosophy, religion, the sciences, and psychology as you match the modern thoughts on the right with their Greek counterparts on the left. The first one has been completed for you.

Greek Thought	**Modern Thought**

__B__ 1. Plato attempted to define justice and the ideal state.

_____ 2. Socrates suggested doing wrong damaged the soul.

_____ 3. The Socratic method is based on raising and answering questions.

_____ 4. Plato discussed the will, the appetites, and the rational parts of human beings.

_____ 5. Socrates stressed the importance of self-examination and maintaining the health of the soul.

_____ 6. Plato stressed the importance of a country's developing an educated constituency.

_____ 7. Aristotle thought individuals followed "built-in" patterns of development.

_____ 8. Aristotle believed happiness could be found only when one avoided extremes.

A. Democracies acknowledge the importance of educating their citizens.

B. Modern constitutions and laws attempt to ensure justice and create the best possible societies.

C. Scientists devise and test a question or hypothesis in conducting research.

D. Modern self-help books assist one in examining the self and maintaining emotional health.

E. Modern religions believe doing wrong brings negative personal consequences.

F. Developmental psychology and genetics both assume individuals have some "built-in" characteristics.

G. Psychologists discuss the id, the ego, and the superego in attempting to understand human beings.

H. Alcoholics Anonymous, Overeaters Anonymous, and other "Anonymous" groups suggest extremes in behavior can be unhealthy and cause pain and unhappiness in oneself and in others.

The Meaning of Life

Develop your own philosophy on the meaning of life and the nature of goodness, justice, and truth by answering the following opinion questions. Then organize your thoughts into a one- to three-page essay explaining your theory of reality. Write your essay on your own paper.

1. Socrates and Plato both believed that people were naturally good. What do you think?

   _____

   _____

   _____

2. Socrates suggested that all evil was the result of ignorance because virtue is knowledge, and those who know what is right will act right. What do you think?

   _____

   _____

   _____

3. Aristotle thought only upper-class adult males could obtain true intellectual and moral excellence and that women, children, manual laborers, and non-Greeks should, therefore, not be allowed to vote. What do you think?

   _____

   _____

   _____

4. How do you define *truth*? _____

   _____

5. How do you define *justice*? _____

   _____

6. How do you define *goodness*? _____

   _____

7. What does it mean to you to be human? How do human beings differ from animals?

   _____

   _____

   _____

Joan of Arc

In 1066 a Frenchman named William the Conqueror declared himself king of England and set the stage for the Hundred Years' War, a century-long dispute between England and France that began 300 years after his death. As late as the mid-fourteenth and early fifteenth centuries, William's descendants—now English—continued to claim sovereignty over certain regions of France. The citizens of some French regions accepted the claim. The citizens of other regions declared all of France to be under the authority of French monarchs. Still other French and English citizens thought it best to unite the whole of the two countries under a single crown. These differences of opinion that ignited battles from 1338 until 1453 may have found no satisfactory end had not a 13-year-old French peasant girl heard voices and seen visions that prompted her to unite her country in a final fight to drive out English armies.

Young Joan of Arc did not wish to go to battle and once told a fellow soldier she would rather be home spinning thread with her mother, but she believed God wanted her to save France from the English. She believed this so strongly that she spoke boldly of her mission to captains, priests, and princes even though she was nothing more than a teenage peasant girl. Her speeches were so persuasive, in fact, that she convinced the Dauphin, a man who would later be crowned king of France, that she should be granted an entire army to command in an attempt to defeat the English. Through bravery, courage, and persistence, Joan of Arc was able to lead armies to victory in battle after battle. Although Joan was put to death before her twentieth birthday on charges of witchcraft, for wearing boys' clothing, and declaring allegiance to God rather than to the church, France gained its independence thanks to the leadership of a determined young peasant girl who heard voices.

Tell about a teenager you know or have heard about who has made a significant contribution to society.

From Cornfield to Battlefield

Learn how the persistence of a peasant girl took her from the fields of her family farm to the battlefields of the Hundred Years' War as you practice interpreting the time line below by answering the questions on the following page.

1066 William the Conqueror takes over the throne in England and sets the stage for the Hundred Years' War.

1338 England's King Edward III declares himself king of France, and the Hundred Years' War officially begins.

1412 Joan of Arc is born in Domrémy, France.

1424 Twelve-year-old Joan of Arc hears a voice that says she will restore peace to France and protect the prince, called the Dauphin, until he can be crowned king.

1426 Joan's father is terrified by a dream in which his daughter dresses like a boy and joins the army.

1428 Joan visits relatives in Vaucouleurs, France, where a small band of soldiers is stationed. While there, she tells Commander Robert de Baudricourt about her mission and requests a soldier escort to speak with Dauphin. The commander laughs at the 16-year-old peasant girl who hears voices.

1428 Upon her return home from Vaucouleurs, Joan finds her town has been burned to the ground.

1429 Joan returns to Vaucouleurs to speak with Commander Baudricourt again as the city of Orleans is under siege by English troops. Convinced by one of his trusted soldiers who has faith in Joan, the commander gives Joan a horse and two escorts so that she can go to speak with the Dauphin.

1429 Joan and her escorts travel 400 miles on horseback to reach the Dauphin's castle. Once there, the Dauphin meets with Joan and agrees to give her command of a number of soldiers because the war is at a desperate stage.

1429-
1430 Dressed in boys' clothing and carrying a banner that becomes a symbol of hope to the men who fight under her lead, Joan of Arc wins many battles. Finally Joan of Arc is captured.

1429 Joan attends the crowning of the Dauphin as Charles VII, king of France.

1431 Joan is questioned by priests and burned at the stake as a witch for wearing boys' clothes and answering to the authority of God above that of the church.

1453 Although a formal treaty is never signed, fighting of the Hundred Years' War ends. France maintains its boundaries thanks to Joan's victories and those she inspired even after her death.

1455 Joan of Arc's family convinces the pope of Rome to reopen Joan's case. Twenty-five years after she was burned at the stake, priests, farmers, dukes, and lords all testify on her behalf, and Joan of Arc is found innocent of witchcraft.

1756-
1946 Joan of Arc is the subject of numerous famous plays, poems, songs, paintings, and biographies.

1920 Joan is declared a saint by Pope Benedict XV.

1. William the Conqueror was king of England 300 years before the start of the Hundred Years' War. How could his claim to the English crown have anything to do with the conflict?

    _____

    _____

    _____

2. How old was Joan of Arc when she died? _____

3. For how many years was Joan of Arc engaged in warfare?_____

4. (a) Why doesn't Captain Robert de Baudricourt provide Joan with an escort to the Dauphin's court in 1428? _____

    _____

    (b) Why does he give in to her request the next year? _____

    _____

5. Does the Hundred Years' War end before or after Joan's death? _____

6. Why is Joan of Arc put to death?_____

    _____

7. Why is Joan of Arc considered a national heroine in France today? _____

    _____

8. In what year was the Dauphin crowned King Charles VII? _____

9. It has been argued that Joan of Arc is the mother of French nationalism. What might be meant by this claim?

    _____

    _____

    _____

10. In addition to saving France from English rule, Joan of Arc has influenced history throughout the ages in other ways as well. In what way might this be?

    _____

    _____

    _____

Name _____

Napoleon Bonaparte

On August 15, 1769, on the small island of Corsica outside of France, a baby boy was born who would grow up to become perhaps the greatest military genius of all time. Napoleon Bonaparte began his military career at the age of ten, when his father enrolled him in French military school. By 1785 he was commissioned a second lieutenant in an artillery brigade of the French army and by 1799, at the age of 30, he overthrew the French government and declared himself the leader of France. He created a new constitution and instituted the Napoleonic Code, which ensured all citizens of the inalienable rights that had been bitterly fought for in the French Revolution. The medieval age in which those who had more power or more money enjoyed different laws and freedoms than peasants and common workers was over.

In 1804 Napoleon Bonaparte became Napoleon I when he transformed the republic of France into an empire and crowned himself emperor. Although he cost the French hundreds of thousands of lives in his conquests of new lands and finally lost to the joined forces of four European countries at the Battle of Waterloo, Napoleon is considered a hero in France and a military genius by military scholars all over the world. Napoleon was so popular, even after being exiled to the island of Elba after his first defeat, that he roused his country to war conquests again by escaping from his place of exile, returning to France, and organizing a new army.

However, Napoleon changed the world through more than just his military genius. Even though ruling as a dictator himself, he introduced to France and all his conquered lands such enlightened principles as equal protection under the law, universal male suffrage, centrally administered school systems, freedom of religion, and a written bill of rights. Many modern-day political, legal, tax, and banking systems are based on the daring ideas of that little boy who grew to be the world's greatest military genius.

What personality traits do people who become immensely popular with the public seem to have in common? _____

_____

Name _____

The Power of Personality

Napoleon had character traits that contributed to both his rise to power and his eventual downfall. Read about Napoleon in an encyclopedia and/or biographies. Then tell how each of the following personality traits could benefit Napoleon in motivating troops, conquering enemies, and gaining popularity among the common people. Next tell how each trait could impede his quest for power. The first one has been done for you.

Character Trait Napoleon was . . .	**Benefit**	**Hindrance**
1. very insecure	made him very driven to prove himself by conquering more and more lands	made him unable to accept that some odds were impossible
2. very power hungry		
3. quite charming		
4. unable to relax		
5. intensely loyal to family		
6. hungry for public approval and legendary status		
7. never satisfied		
8. very driven to accomplish goals		

If I Were Emperor . . .

Napoleon seemed to have the world in his hands, if only for a brief period of time. What would you do in such a situation? Write an essay about all the changes you would institute in the world if you were in charge of absolutely everything.

_____

_____

_____

_____

_____

_____

_____

_____

_____

_____

_____

_____

_____

_____

_____

_____

_____

_____

_____

_____

_____

_____

_____

Wolfgang Amadeus Mozart

In 1762 a 6-year-old boy and his 11-year-old sister hopped onto a stagecoach in Austria and set out with their father for a number of cities throughout Europe. The children were Wolfgang Mozart and his sister Nannerl, and the purpose of their travels was to entertain kings and queens, princes, and archbishops with their extraordinary skill of piano playing. Child prodigies were celebrated then much like rock stars are today. Wolfgang's father wished for both of his children to bring a little money into their current household and for his son, who would need employment as an adult, to become well-known enough to land a job in some European court in later years.

In those days European musicians were not considered respectable artists but servants of various courts. Wolfgang's father was an assistant concert master at the court of the Salzburg archbishop and a fine composer and violinist. Still, he ate with the servants, performed only when called upon, and composed only those symphonies and operas commissioned to him by the court. His son would grow up to want something different.

Wolfgang Amadeus Mozart became not only one of the greatest musical geniuses the world has ever known, but he also helped to change the way artists would be viewed in society. Unwilling to restrict his creativity to only those projects commissioned by a single court of employment, Mozart worked as a "freelance" musician. He composed operas, symphonies, concertos, and chamber music; he gave music lessons; he accompanied singers; he arranged the music of other composers; and he performed for famous and common persons alike. Although he was not very successful financially due to the economic climate in France preceding the French Revolution, Mozart's insistence on working outside of the confines of the regal system liberated musicians and other artists who were to follow him.

Are there any social "rules" that you would rather not follow?_____

_____

Name _____

Boy Genius

Read about Mozart in an encyclopedia and/or in biographies from your school library and then answer the following true-false questions that attempt to explain why Wolfgang Mozart is considered by many musical historians Western history's greatest musician. The first one has been done for you.

Mozart is known as one of the greatest musicians the world has ever known because . . .

T (F) 1. . . . he composed music very slowly, painstakingly thinking out every note before committing it to paper.
False—Mozart worked at an amazing speed and could compose final-draft quality pieces directly on an instrument without first writing down a single note.

T F 2. . . . he lived to such an old age that he was able to write over 600 pieces of music before he died.

T F 3. . . . he was so well received by royalty and common people alike during his lifetime.

T F 4. . . . he adopted the positive aspects of other contemporary composers such as Johann Christian Bach and Franz Joseph Haydn.

T F 5. . . . he had an uncanny "sense" of music. He had perfect pitch, could imitate the techniques of others perfectly, taught himself to play the violin, and could record on paper a full musical score that he had never seen but had only heard performed long before.

T F 6. . . . he displayed a remarkable understanding of the psychology of men and women in the operas he wrote.

T F 7. . . . his music contains such a strong emotional content.

T F 8. . . . he was already well-known throughout Europe before he reached adulthood for his ability to play a piece of music put before him no matter how difficult. He was also known for his ability to pass with ease "musical tests" given him by famous musicians around the continent.

T F 9. . . . he stayed in Vienna all of his adult life so that he could establish a solid reputation as the court composer of the Viennese court.

T F 10. . . . his music continues to inspire musicians and music lovers more than 200 years after his death.

A Few Notes About Music

Define the following styles and forms of music and musical compositions in complete sentences by locating them in a dictionary and rephrasing your findings in your own words.

1. *Classical music:* _____
   _____

2. *Baroque music:* _____
   _____

3. *Opera:* _____
   _____

4. *Chant:* _____
   _____

5. *Chamber music:* _____
   _____

6. *Serenade:* _____
   _____

7. *Folk music:* _____
   _____

8. *Symphony:* _____
   _____

9. *Minuet:* _____
   _____

10. *Sonata:* _____
    _____

11. *Concerto:* _____
    _____

12. *Requiem:* _____
    _____

Lucretia Mott

Lucretia Mott did not set out to become the mother of the women's rights movement. Rather she intended to see slaves legally set free. Born in 1793 when George Washington was still president of the United States, Lucretia lived in a time when slavery was an accepted part of the Southern economy, but Mrs. Mott objected to the entire institution. She objected so strongly that she spoke against slavery at all-male gatherings and even formed one of the country's first female political organizations—the Female Anti-Slavery Society.

Much of Lucretia's boldness in speaking out on the abolition issue can be credited to her Quaker upbringing. Not only did Quakers believe slavery was wrong, but they also believed women should be able to speak publicly the same as men. So Lucretia Mott became an ordained minister of the Quaker church, and she was sought as a powerful preacher at meetings of Quaker Friends all over the new United States.

However, the non-Quaker world was not so ready to listen to the views of a woman in the 1800s. When Lucretia was elected as a delegate to an antislavery convention in England, she and the other female delegates were not allowed to participate in discussions or to vote on resolutions. Lucretia realized that if she were to make headway on her agenda to free the slaves, she would have to promote the rights of women as well. In 1848 she and Elizabeth Stanton organized the first women's convention, and Mrs. Mott continued to work for both causes for the remainder of her life.

Lucretia Mott did not see the complete liberation of either women or blacks, but she did live to see slavery outlawed and her own words respected by nearly everyone she encountered including the 20 presidents that she lived to see take office before her death at the age of 87. Thanks to the persistence of Mrs. Mott and others, women and minorities demanded attention in the United States. Laws concerning their rights were eventually passed.

What goals still need to be accomplished before women, minorities, and all U.S. citizens are to share equal rights? _____

_____

_____

Lucretia Mott Accomplished a Lot

In the following paragraphs about the life and accomplishments of Lucretia Mott, the **introductory sentence** is missing. Compose an introductory sentence for each paragraph by determining the **main idea** of the sentences included.

1. _____

_____

As a child, she would imitate the speeches of adults who gathered in her home to discuss current-day issues with her parents. By the time she was 28, she was a Quaker preacher. Throughout her lifetime she traveled around the world speaking on behalf of the rights of both women and blacks. Even into her feeble twilight years, when she attended any event, she was asked to address the audience with a few words.

2. _____

_____

She invited everyone from former slaves to presidents of the United States into her home to share a meal. She entertained foreign diplomats, important business people, extended family members, famous authors, philosophers, historians, artists, and not-so-famous starry-eyed admirers who had heard of her from afar. She was once introduced at a gathering with the following words, "This is Mrs. Lucretia Mott. Mrs. Mott is a great abolitionist, but she's a fine cook too." (Daniel Neall as quoted in *Lucretia Mott: Gentle Warrior* by Dorothy Sterling, Doubleday, New York, 1964)

3. _____

_____

Some Quakers shunned her because she identified with the liberal Hicks faction and mingled too much with the outside world. Men scolded her often for assuming she was their equal. Politicians squirmed when she demanded blacks not only be freed from the bondage of slavery, but welcomed in all public and private gatherings of whites. Yet, by her golden years, her calm and persistent manner had won over the world which applauded her at every appearance and wished her well.

4. _____

_____

She and her husband James raised six children. James accompanied her on all of her travels and accomplished great reforms in education and minority relations himself. There were always aunts and uncles, cousins, siblings, or grandparents around the Mott household. Family members helped raise funds, entertain guests, and organize events. The causes of Lucretia were also the causes of her family.

Lucretia's Contemporaries

Lucretia Mott did not work alone for the freedom of the black slave or the equality of women. Locate in an encyclopedia the following reformers who were contemporaries of Mrs. Mott and then match their names with their accomplishments. The first one has been done for you.

Sojourner Truth	William Lloyd Garrison	Frederick Douglass
Elizabeth Stanton	Susan B. Anthony	Abraham Lincoln
Ernestine Rose	Lucy Stone	James Mott
Charles Dickens	Ralph Waldo Emerson	The Hutchinsons

William Lloyd Garrison   1. Encouraged by Mrs. Mott to speak more forcefully for his cause, this publisher of *The Liberator* took his friend's advice and issued the first U.S. newspaper to call for the immediate and unconditional abolition of slavery.

_____ 2. This fellow female preacher, who was a former slave, had a remarkable ability to hush hecklers and mesmerize a crowd.

_____ 3. After a visit with Lucretia, this famous British author wrote *American Notes,* which strongly denounced slavery.

_____ 4. Although Quakers do not normally attend concerts, Lucretia broke with tradition to listen to this musical family who toured the country singing antislavery songs and inviting blacks to their concerts.

_____ 5. This women's rights activist worked with Lucretia to organize a convention in Seneca Falls, New York.

_____ 6. This women's rights activist is best known for her role in the woman's suffrage movement.

_____ 7. This famous poet and philosopher, who wrote in favor of equal rights for all, once visited with Lucretia in her home.

_____ 8. Lucretia's husband was active in abolition organizations and the formation of schools for females and blacks.

_____ 9. This U.S. president issued the Emancipation Proclamation.

_____ 10. This abolitionist and women's rights activist was one of the first women in the country to graduate from college.

_____ 11. This black man escaped from slavery to become an incredible orator who became a strong leader in the abolition and women's rights movements.

_____ 12. Along with Susan B. Anthony and Elizabeth Stanton, this woman founded the National Suffrage Association.

John Davison Rockefeller and Descendants

John Davison Rockefeller (1839-1937) changed the world on the following three fronts.

Business Practices That Prompted Antitrust Legislation
By 1878 John D. Rockefeller owned an oil company that was very powerful. He accomplished that by buying out other oil companies, bullying railroads into not transporting other companies' oil, and uniting numerous businesses under a single trust umbrella. That umbrella was his Standard Oil Company. In fact Standard Oil enjoyed over 90% of all oil refinery business in the United States. Rockefeller caused such an uproar by eliminating competitors and controlling the entire oil market, that several antitrust acts were enacted, a Federal Trade Commission was established, and the Supreme Court ordered his company to be divided into separate corporations. Since the rise of Standard Oil and other huge conglomerates in the early 1900s, the United States courts have continued to grapple with how to define what is and is not fair in the corporate world.

Establishment of the Rockefeller Foundation
At the peak of his career, John D. Rockefeller claimed a personal fortune of one billion dollars. He contributed more than $550 million of this sum to philanthropic causes, establishing the Rockefeller Foundation, the General Education Board, and other private institutions. The Rockefeller Foundation, which was established to "promote the well-being of mankind throughout the world," continues to make grants, develop programs, and fund research for the betterment of humanity.

The Rockefeller Family
John D. Rockefeller also steered history by producing heirs who have been influential in politics, economics, and human affairs worldwide. Read about some of their accomplishments on the next page.

In your opinion, if a person is going to use money for the benefit of humanity, does it matter how he or she acquires the wealth? Why or why not? _____

_____

The Rockefeller Clan

John D. Rockefeller produced influential children who produced influential children who produced influential children. Read about John D. Rockefeller's heirs in an encyclopedia to assist you in matching their names with their accomplishments. The first one has been done for you.

__D__ 1. Nelson Rockefeller

_____ 2. John D. Rockefeller, III

_____ 3. David Rockefeller

_____ 4. John D. Rockefeller, IV

_____ 5. John D. Rockefeller, Jr.

_____ 6. Laurance S. Rockefeller

_____ 7. Winthrop Rockefeller

A. (1915-   ) An influential financier, he served as president of Chase Manhattan Bank before retiring in 1981.

B. (1874-1960) Upon his father's retirement, he headed the Rockefeller Industries. He also supervised the construction of the Rockefeller Center and donated land for the site of the United Nations complex.

C. (1912-1973) Governor of Arkansas from 1967-1971, he also served as director of the Rockefeller Brothers Fund for many years.

D. (1908-1979) Republican governor of New York for four terms, he was also vice president under Gerald Ford and head of many boards and committees under various presidents.

E. (1906-1978) With his four brothers, he established the Rockefeller Brothers Fund, which finances education and economics projects. He also supported the arts and recognized distinguished service in government and five other fields with the annual $10,000 Rockefeller Public Service Award.

F. (1910-   ) He financially supports land and resource conservation, cancer research, and new technology development. He donated the land for the site of the Virgin Islands National Park.

G. (1937-) As an influential politician, he was elected U.S. senator in 1985.

The Rockefeller Foundation

The Rockefeller Foundation, with a $100 million annual budget, establishes grants for projects in specific program areas. Under each program area below record the letter accompanying a foundation accomplishment that fits under its umbrella of goals. The first one has been done for you.

Program Areas

Agricultural Sciences

____ ____ ____ ____ ____

Arts and Humanities

A ____ ____ ____ ____ ____

Population and Health Sciences

____ ____ ____ ____ ____

Equal Opportunities

____ ____ ____ ____ ____ ____

A. 1940—The Boston Symphony Orchestra receives a grant to establish the Berkshire Music Center.

B. 1943—An agricultural research and production project is started in Mexico.

C. 1944—A grant develops the Princeton Office of Population Research.

D. 1950—Grants establish numerous genetic research centers.

E. 1954—Grants help found the American Shakespeare Festival.

F. 1955—India is aided in establishing a family-planning program.

G. 1960—Financial aid is provided to university presses translating Latin-American literature into English.

H. 1961—The Southern Regional Council receives a $250,000 grant to assist in improving race relations in the South.

I. 1963—Grants are provided to increase the enrollment of black students in colleges.

J. 1967—A grant is provided to the NAACP Legal Defense and Education Fund to pioneer a program on protection of basic rights.

K. 1970—The Rockefeller Foundation field scientist Dr. Norman Borlaug receives the Nobel Peace Prize for introducing modern farming techniques to developing countries.

L. 1973—Grants support women's studies at various colleges.

M. 1977—An international network of biomedical researchers is developed to study "great neglected diseases."

N. 1981—Composer Philip Glass is financially rewarded for his work in music.

O. 1984—Support is provided for plant genetic engineering.

P. 1985—African-, Asian-, and Latin-American scientists are recruited to assist with biomedical research projects in contraception introduction (fits under two program areas).

Q. 1987—U.S. independent film artists are financially supported.

R. 1990—Grants support Hispanic literature.

S. 1991—Projects intended to create nutritionally improved rice varieties are funded.

T. 1995—Strides are made in increasing employment in poor, urban communities in the United States.

U. 1997—Young social scientists work on agricultural and rural development projects in developing countries' universities and research centers.

Norman Borlaug

Norman Borlaug is the father of the Green Revolution. Norman Borlaug is one of only three living recipients of the Nobel Peace Prize. Norman Borlaug is the savior of literally billions of lives worldwide. Norman Borlaug is an American. Yet Norman Borlaug is hardly a household name in America. Why?

For all of his adult life, Norman Borlaug has had the goal of stamping out starvation all over the world by introducing modern farming methods to developing countries. Funded by the World Bank, the Rockefeller Foundation, and other government and private groups, he has cultivated high-yield breeds of wheat and corn and taught people all around the globe how to get a large volume of food from a small plot of land. In the process he has saved countless human lives from starvation and unnumbered acres of forests and plains from the slash-and-burn techniques that preceded his high-yield methods.

Initially the world was thankful. After India, Pakistan, and Turkey greatly increased their annual crop production, Mr. Borlaug was awarded the Nobel Prize for Peace in 1970. Then environmentalists became concerned. An ample food supply seemed to open the way for population growth, and it appeared the world could not sustain any more people. Also, Borlaug's methods relied on the use of chemical fertilizers, and environmentalists disputed the excessive use of chemicals in farming.

Mr. Borlaug answered that statistics suggested high-yield agriculture actually reduces population growth by destroying feudal systems which encouraged high birthrates. He explained the difference between fertilizers and pesticides and showed the significant difference in destruction caused by each. Some environmentalists returned to Borlaug's camp. Still, when he wished to introduce his methods to the nations of Africa, he no longer had the support of any of the government or private foundations he had relied on in the past. Norman Borlaug entered virtual retirement.

Then in 1984 when Mr. Borlaug was 71 years old, he received a call from a wealthy Japanese individual named Ryoichi Sasakawa. Mr. Sasakawa and the former United States president Jimmy Carter wanted to make real Borlaug's dream of relieving hunger on the African continent. Though a long way from success in his goal and still an unknown in his own country, Norman Borlaug continues to work with fellow agriculture experts, undaunted by the hurdles of social, political, and economic realities that interfere with efforts to end world hunger.

He's Made a Difference: Is It a Positive One?

Answer the following questions in complete sentences, based on the reading.

1. Why did Norman Borlaug win the Nobel Peace Prize in 1970?_____

_____

2. In his Nobel Peace Prize acceptance speech, Norman Borlaug warned that if the "population monster" were not "tamed" by the year 2000, starvation would befall more people than at any time in the history of humankind. Why do Norman Borlaug's opponents think he is contributing to population growth? How does Mr. Borlaug answer his opponents? _____

_____

_____

_____

3. The Green Revolution refers to high-yield farming methods that have greatly increased the yields of crops in developing countries where they have been implemented. Why do Green Revolution supporters encourage high-yield farming? Why have some environmentalists discouraged the "Revolution"? _____

_____

_____

_____

4. Do you personally think it is a good idea to teach developing nations modern farming techniques using high-yield crops? Why or why not? _____

_____

_____

_____

_____

_____

_____

_____

Name _____

Understanding Agriculture

Use a dictionary if necessary to help you match the following terms from the field of agriculture with their definitions. The first one has been done for you.

fertilizer	pesticide	chemical
world food supply	integrated pest management	dwarf wheat
high-yield crops	cultivate	genetic engineering

_____fertilizer_____ 1. a chemical or natural product, such as manure, that replaces nutrients already naturally found in the soil; much less toxic than pesticides

_____ 2. This term refers to the ratio of food produced to the world population. Norman Borlaug and others have warned that increases in food production cannot keep up with increases in population at the current rate.

_____ 3. a substance produced in chemistry rather than in nature

_____ 4. This verb means "to foster the growth of."

_____ 5. Although Mr. Borlaug doubts that this new science can increase the world food supply fast enough to match population growth, some people believe that this and biotechnology, or packing more nutrients into foods, will help to feed the world.

_____ 6. chemical or natural compounds used to deter insects from destroying crops

_____ 7. crops that have been specifically cultured to produce a lot of food on a small plot of land

_____ 8. This process allows farmers to use a minimal amount of pesticides by applying them at the most vulnerable time in the cycle of an insect's life.

_____ 9. This high-yield grain first cultivated by Norman Borlaug in Mexico is the wheat that much of the world relies on today.

Gavrilo Princip

On June 28, 1914, Gavrilo Princip, a 19-year-old-boy who identified with a secret Serbian terrorist group called the Black Hand, killed Archduke Franz Ferdinand, the heir apparent to the Austrian throne. His action prompted Austria-Hungary to declare war on Serbia. This in turn, prompted allies of each country to join in the fighting until nations from all around the globe were engaged in the first world war. The conflict killed over 47 million people around the world in the course of four years.

Europe in the late 1880s was ripe for war. The Congress of Vienna that ended the reign of Napoleon created conflicts between many Europeans. It accomplished this by subjecting smaller regions to the rule of neighboring states instead of dividing the continent into individual nations with common languages, politics, and ethnic ties. In addition to that problem, the Industrial Revolution's enormous outpouring of goods necessitated the establishment of trading partners. The jealous competition for colonies in Africa made the countries of Europe distrustful of one another. Individual nations built up huge standing armies and banned together to form alliances in case of conflict.

Austria-Hungary angered Serbia by declaring political authority over Bosnia and Herzegovina, preventing the formation of a Greater Serbia. This resulted in the assassination of the archduke of Austria. The assassination set the entire world on the course of a long and bloody war that would take place on land and water on numerous fronts around the globe. In addition to the devastating destruction directly caused by the war, the resulting Treaty of Versailles, which burdened Germany with both the guilt and the economic responsibility of World War I, set the stage for World War II. Gavrilo Princip's decision to murder Franz Ferdinand initiated a chain of events that would not stop reeling for decades.

Describe a situation where you have noticed the "domino effect" in which a single decision became responsible for a great number of happenings:_____

_____

_____

_____

The Archduke's Assassination

Should fate have been on his side, Nedjelko Cabrinovic, and not Gavrilo Princip, would have been the man that changed the world by precipitating the beginning of the first world war by assassinating the archduke of Austria-Hungary. Read the following true account of the assassination of Franz Ferdinand and then number the events listed on the following page in the order in which they took place. The first event has been numbered for you.

On June 28, 1914, Archduke Franz Ferdinand from Austria was scheduled to visit the city of Sarajevo, Bosnia. Although the general public welcomed the visit, Colonel Dimitrijevic of the Black Hand organization saw it as an opportunity to murder the heir apparent to the Austria-Hungarian crown. The Black Hand was an organization of Serbian nationalists that carried out assassinations and terrorist activities in protest of Austria's political annexing of Bosnia and Herzegovina.

Colonel Dimitrijevic recruited three men, including Gavrilo Princip, at a cafe to carry bombs and guns into Sarajevo weeks before the archduke's visit. The rest of the Black Hand did not officially endorse the assassination plan because the Serbian government contained so many Black Hand members that the Austrians might blame the government for the murder. Men were sent to Sarajevo to cancel the order, but the attempt to dissuade the assassins was half-hearted. Realizing the assassination attempt would still be made, the Serbian government sent a representative to warn the Austria-Hungarian government of the plan, but the Austria-Hungarian representative did not understand the somewhat veiled warning.

So, on the day of the archduke's visit, as he sat in the backseat of an open car that drove down the streets of Sarajevo, Gavrilo Princip, Nedjelko Cabrinovic, Trifko Grabez, and four other men who had joined the mission (including two 17-year-olds) stood at various locations along the streets of the archduke's scheduled travel path. When the archduke's car passed the first would-be assassin, he did nothing. When the car passed Nedjelko Cabrinovic, he threw a bomb, which Archduke Ferdinand deflected with his arm so as to protect his wife who sat beside him. The bomb exploded behind the car and the archduke and his party continued on to the city hall, their destination. Mr. Cabrinovic took cyanide and jumped into a river. The cyanide, however, proved old and the river shallow, and Mr. Cabrinovic was captured alive and arrested.

The remaining would-be assassins did not know where to stand next. The archduke's scheduled route following his city-hall stop would certainly be altered in light of the first attempt. The men scattered about as the archduke visited with the mayor of the city. Gavrilo Princip had just walked out of a sandwich shop where he had grabbed some lunch when the archduke's car made a sudden stop just in front of the store. The driver realized he had deviated from the agreed-upon alternative route and was about to turn around when Gavrilo pulled a gun from his coat and shot both the archduke and his wife. The two victims died shortly thereafter, but Princip's cyanide was of the same batch as his friend's and he only became ill when he took it. Like Cabrinovic, he was captured by the crowds and arrested for the assassination of an archduke, whom a bomb alone could not destroy.

Chain of Events

Write a number in the blank space beside each happening to accurately order the chain of events that resulted in the death of Archduke Franz Ferdinand and his wife Sophia on June 28, 1914. The first one has been done for you.

_____ Colonel Dimitrijevic recruits three men from a cafe to assassinate the archduke in Sarajevo.

___1___ Austria-Hungry annexes Bosnia and Herzegovina.

_____ With his own arm, the archduke deflects a bomb that is thrown at his car.

_____ Franz Ferdinand's car stops in front of a sandwich shop to turn around when the driver realizes he has made a wrong turn.

_____ The Black Hand organization is formed.

_____ Nedjelko Cabrinovic fails a suicide attempt, is accosted by the crowd, and arrested.

_____ The Black Hand sends representatives to Sarajevo to cancel the assassination order.

_____ The archduke of Austria schedules a trip to Sarajevo, Bosnia.

_____ The Serbian government warns the Austria-Hungarian government about the Black Hand's plan to assassinate Franz Ferdinand.

_____ Gavrilo Princip steps into a sandwich shop for lunch.

_____ Gavrilo Princip is arrested for the assassination of Franz and Sophia Ferdinand, when his suicide attempt falls.

_____ Gavrilo Princip shoots Franz Ferdinand and his wife, Sophia, when he looks up from eating a sandwich and chatting with a friend to find the archduke's car stopping directly in front of him.

The Big Three

Winston Churchill, Joseph Stalin, and Franklin Roosevelt

Through conferencing and military action, Winston Churchill of Great Britain, Franklin Roosevelt of the United States, and Joseph Stalin of the USSR put an end to the most destructive conflict in world history when they defeated Adolf Hitler in World War II. In the process, "The Big Three" redefined the world's balance of power and set the stage for the cold war that would dominate relations between communist and democratic nations for decades to come. Each man played his own unique role in the accomplishments.

Winston Churchill

On September 3, 1939, World War II officially began when France and Britain declared war on Germany in response to its invasion of Poland. By the spring of 1940, Germany had already defeated Denmark, Norway, the Netherlands, Belgium, and France. Since the USSR was still friendly with Germany at the time and the United States had not yet entered the conflict, the British—for the time being—faced Germany alone. From August of 1940 through May of 1941, the Germans bombed London and other cities 71 times in an attempt to destroy English morale and persuade the British to surrender. Winston Churchill's courageous leadership and bulldog determination in the face of his opponent's relentless raids fortified his countrymen and kept Germany at bay until help arrived. Churchill's willingness to meet with Franklin Roosevelt on numerous occasions to plan strategies and write declarations against any nation's unwelcome occupation of another country ultimately helped defeat Hitler and shape the postwar world.

Joseph Stalin

On June 22, 1941, Germany broke an agreement with Stalin and invaded the USSR. Churchill immediately accepted Stalin as an ally, and he was invited to two major conferences with Churchill and Roosevelt. Initially he agreed to free elections in Eastern Europe, the establishment of the United Nations, and the division of Germany that helped shape the postwar world. But his later decision to renege on the free elections issue established a cold war atmosphere between the Eastern communist bloc and the nations of the West.

Franklin Roosevelt

On December 7, 1941, Japan invaded Pearl Harbor, and the United States officially entered into World War II. Already having aided France and Britain financially for many months, Roosevelt was now able to influence strategy and determine the course of action necessary to put an end to Hitler's aggressions. His goal was not an easy one. He had to build up a large army quickly and set the United States on a wartime economy. He needed to determine the logistics of men and materials in a global conflict and keep the American people happy with his decision to join the war in the first place. Although he died before either the Germans or the Japanese surrendered, Roosevelt could see by the end of his days that the war would soon end.

World War II cost the world over $1 trillion and 60 million lives including 6 million who were killed in concentration camps. The USSR and the United States did not enter the conflict until their own lands were attacked. Do you think the war would have been shorter and less costly if these two nations had entered the conflict earlier? Why or why not?

_____

_____

_____

Wars cause death and destruction on an unbelievably grand scale. When is war justified, if ever? Is it ever inevitable? If not, what are the alternatives to war?

_____

_____

_____

Stalin, The Despot

Joseph Stalin may have assisted Roosevelt and Churchill in defeating Hitler, but he was not an especially nice person in his own right. Read about his approach to dealing with conflicts in his own country and then offer an alternative approach to each problem. The first one has been done for you.

The Conflict	Stalin's Action	Alternative Action
workers and peasants in the USSR were underpaid and ill-treated	organized a bank holdup to expropriate funds	attempt political change through organized campaign
agricultural production could not keep up with hunger needs of the people	took grain from peasants in Siberia to feed people in Russia	
food production continued to lag	took food from peasants nationwide; millions were displaced or died	
needed people to support his regime	established the KGB, political secret police to frighten people into submission	
needed support of his political decisions	Citizens who opposed Stalin were jailed, killed, or deported to concentration camps.	
desired control of more land	did not allow free elections in Eastern Europe following World War II	

Mohandas Gandhi

On January 30, 1948, a man, whose entire 79 years on earth were defined by a steadfast insistence on nonviolence, was killed by gunshots. Yet his influence on the world did not end on the day of his passing. The example of Mohandas Gandhi's life has motivated numerous reformers to effect social change through peaceful means.

Mohandas Gandhi was born into a traditional Hindu family that respected all life forms and opposed violence. People of all classes and religions were welcomed into the Gandhi home. This background of tolerance affected every aspect of Gandhi's life.

After earning a degree in law from a college in London and gaining employment as a lawyer in South Africa, Gandhi became outraged at the treatment of Indians and blacks in the English-ruled African nation. He spent 21 years in South Africa helping to outlaw unjust tax and registration rules that affected people of color. He did this by writing newspaper articles, defying the government, and uniting masses behind his cause.

In 1915 Gandhi returned to his homeland and applied the system of passive resistance he had developed in South Africa to unjust situations in India. This theory of *satyagraha*, or "steadfastness in truth" led Gandhi to boycott British goods, organize labor strikes, lead marches, endure hunger strikes, and pray fervently. He also defied unjust laws and risked and encountered arrest on frequent occasions.

Gandhi's moral convictions and persistent adherence to *satyagraha* motivated others to join him. Without ever raising a rifle or even holding a public office, Gandhi led masses in a campaign of nonviolent resistance that ultimately freed India from British rule and improved the social status of India's lowest classes.

Nathuram Godse assassinated Gandhi in 1948, while Gandhi was on his way to prayers. The lessons of his life, however, did not die with the man. Nonviolent movements based on participants' steadfast insistence on truth and justice continue to effect change worldwide.

Tell about a time you effected change by standing up boldly for what you knew to be right without resorting to violence.

Steadfastness in Truth

Men and women through this century have respected the philosophy of Gandhi that insisted on change accomplished without violence. Martin Luther King, Jr., once said of Gandhi, "He lived, thought, and acted inspired by the vision of humanity evolving toward a world of peace and harmony. We may ignore Gandhi at our own risk."

Listed below are names of individuals who stood their ground for the sake of justice and truth. Match the passive resisters on the left with their bold actions on the right. The first one has been done for you.

__C__ 1. Rosa Parks

_____ 2. Muhammad Ali

_____ 3. Martin Luther King, Jr.

_____ 4. Eugene Debs

_____ 5. César Chavez

_____ 6. Anne Brown

_____ 7. Mother Jones

_____ 8. Jackie Robinson

A. This woman refused to go on stage in her lead role position in the Broadway musical *Porgy and Bess* unless blacks would be allowed in the "all white" performance hall along with whites.

B. At the expense of his World Boxing Championship Title (later returned to him) and facing a $10,000 fine and five years in prison, this man refused to fight in Vietnam because of his conviction against war.

C. This black woman faced a jail sentence in 1955 when she refused to give up her seat on a Montgomery, Alabama, public bus to a white passenger.

D. This founder of the first farm workers' union led a nationwide boycott of California table grapes in an effort to achieve fair labor contracts for farmers.

E. This celebrated civil rights leader led marches and sit-ins, addressed crowds with strong, intelligent, and inspiring speeches, and defined passive resistance in America.

F. This five-time candidate for the U.S. presidency was well-respected by friends and foes alike for his polite, firm steadfastness in truth. He was sentenced to 10 years in prison when he spoke against U.S. involvement in World War I. While in prison he ran for president on the Social Democratic Party ticket and won nearly one million votes.

G. This first black professional baseball player in the "white" leagues continued to play with grace and skill as he faced continual prejudice on the baseball circuit.

H. As one of America's most effective union organizers, this person stood up for miners who endured unsafe working conditions and inadequate pay.

A Full Life

Following are random facts from the extraordinary life of Mohandas Gandhi. Place each specific fact under the more general statements about the full life of the father of passive resistance. The first one has been placed for you.

Fact One: Millions of followers called Gandhi *Mahatma* or Great Soul.

Fact Two: Gandhi never prosecuted those who beat or attacked him.

Fact Three: Gandhi ate no meat, fruit, or starches.

Fact Four: In later life, Gandhi made his own simple clothes.

Fact Five: To show that the menial labor of the "untouchable" caste was important and nothing to be ashamed of, Gandhi often engaged in such tasks as gardening and even toilet cleaning.

Fact Six: When the "untouchables" sat apart from others at gatherings where Gandhi was to speak, he moved from the front of the gathering to the midst of the "untouchables" and spoke from there.

Fact Seven: Laws requiring blacks and Indians to register and to pay high taxes were dropped in South Africa because of the work of Gandhi.

Fact Eight: The caste system in India began to break down as Gandhi accepted people of all religions and classes and even encouraged women to effect change.

Fact Nine: Gandhi called off passive resistance campaigns on more than one occasion—sometimes in response to violent riots.

Fact Ten: Upon the report of Gandhi's death, the United Nation's flag was flown at half-mast as the whole world mourned the death of a hero.

Fact Eleven: Gandhi actually encouraged Indians to enlist in World War I to assist the British, perhaps in hopes that the British would grant India its freedom following the war.

Fact Twelve: Although Gandhi was sometimes jailed for disregarding unjust laws, he was never kept in bondage for long, because the government feared angering an entire nation which stood behind Gandhi.

Mohandas Gandhi was loved by millions.

   Fact One _____

_____

_____

Mohandas Gandhi lived a simple life.

_____

_____

Mohandas Gandhi achieved change.

_____

_____

Mohandas Gandhi led by example.

_____

_____

_____

Mohandas Gandhi sometimes surprised and even angered followers.

_____   _____

Rachel Carson

If major chemical companies of the early 1960s had their way, Rachel Carson would not have changed the world. She still would have been the first woman to pass the civil service exam in the United States. She still would have intrigued listeners with true stories about sea life explorations on her popular radio program. She still would have been a best-selling and award-winning fiction writer who mesmerized readers with her command of the language and her indisputable scientific accuracy. Yet if chemical companies had their way, Rachel Carson's history-changing work, *Silent Spring*, would have been discredited as ridiculous.

Carson's 1962 book *Silent Spring* warned that the indiscriminate use of pesticides, particularly DDT, was upsetting the balance of nature, killing waterfowl and birds, and even endangering the health of human beings. Chemical companies of the day begged to differ. After all, human beings control nature, so how could an imbalance in nature "control" or threaten human beings? *Silent Spring*, the pesticide industry insisted, was written by a hysterical woman who wildly exaggerated the dangers of DDT use.

Both the public and elected officials were not so quick to dismiss Ms. Carson's work. *Silent Spring* sold over half a million copies, and a television program featured the book and its author. President Kennedy appointed a panel to research the claims of both Rachel and the chemical companies. The panel found the claims of *Silent Spring* indisputable, and Rachel Carson's view began to change the world. Congress held hearings on pesticide use, grassroots environmental groups emerged, and the use of DDT was banned in the United States. In 1970 the government established the Environmental Protection Agency. Rachel Carson had become the mother of what is now known as the environmental movement.

Why do scientists now contend that imbalances in nature can affect human life?

_____

_____

We're Not There Yet

Although Rachel Carson awakened both public and political concern about the environment, there remains much work to be done. The production of pesticides alone has increased 400% since the writing of *Silent Spring*. Explain why each of the following pesticide law "loopholes" makes it difficult to ensure that safe levels of pesticides are used in agriculture. The first one has been done for you.

1. *The loophole:* Pesticides that have been banned for use in the United States can still be manufactured here and sold to other countries for their use.

   The problem: __Environmental concerns have no national boundaries. Upsetting__ __natural balances anywhere in the world affects the entire global environment.__

2. *The loophole:* When the government sets levels for the safe use of pesticides, it takes into account both the potential environmental harm and economic advantage of using the chemical.

   The problem: _____

   _____

3. *The loophole:* Research conducted on the harm of pesticides focuses on adults, although children are much more affected by the chemicals.

   The problem: _____

   _____

4. *The loophole:* It takes five to ten years to remove a pesticide from the market.

   The problem: _____

   _____

5. *The loophole:* Research on pesticides focuses on one chemical at a time, although most are used in combination with others in real-world settings.

   The problem: _____

   _____

6. *The loophole:* Pesticides that are known to cause cancer or reproductive problems in animals are difficult to attribute directly to cancer or reproductive problems in humans.

   The problem: _____

   _____

7. *The loophole:* Agriculture and chemical industry special interest groups indirectly influence research conclusions about the harms and benefits of pesticide usage.

   The problem: _____

   _____

A Quiet World

In *Silent Spring* Rachel Carson imagines a world with no birds. Write a short story with a setting in an imaginary world where there are no animals of any kind. How would life on earth be different without the presence of animals?

_____

_____

_____

_____

_____

_____

_____

_____

_____

_____

_____

_____

_____

_____

_____

_____

_____

_____

_____

_____

Elvis, the Beatles, and the Age of Rock and Roll

In 1953 a recent high school graduate who worked as a truck driver decided to record a few songs as a birthday present for his mother. As he sang and played his guitar, the young man's unique combination of blues, gospel, and country music styles impressed the studio manager. Soon Elvis Presley was recording for the studio's independent label, and a little later, producing major hits for RCA Records. Presley added live performances and movie acting to his resumé, and by the time of his death, he was considered the King of Rock and Roll.

The Beatles, who appeared on the pop music scene ten years after Elvis's first recording session, could claim just as much success. At first the Beatles were only carried on independent labels in the United States for fear that their British sound would not catch on here. But the fabulous four were soon to become the most popular group America had ever known. They had an unprecedented 30 songs reach the Billboard top-ten list from 1964 through 1969. A generation later, when a three-album retrospective of the Beatles was released in 1995, it became one of the fastest-selling recordings in history.

Both Elvis and the Beatles define a profound shift in popular music that overwhelmed the world gradually after 1954. The Golden Age of Rock and Roll was a period of rebellious new ideas in music with an emphasis on both lyrics and beats that appealed to young people and did not attempt to appease critics or the status quo. A victim of its own success, rock and roll soon became a commercial venture, employing professional song writers and session musicians in place of innovative renegades. But the roots of popular music reside in rebellion, and rock and roll refuses to be static. Since the 1950s, rock music has reinvented itself again and again as independent labels introduce new ideas that become mainstream only to be bumped by the innovations of the next independent label sound.

In music, or in other areas of life, is new and fresh always better than tried and true? Why or why not?_____

_____

The Mass Music Movement

Rock music reinvents itself often as mainstream labels look to the work of independent label performers for new trends and talent. Read the time line below to see how popular music has changed throughout the decades. Then devise ten questions based on the time line and write them on your own paper. Trade papers with a classmate and answer each other's questions.

Popular Music in America

1700-1800 As judged by sales of printed music, since radios and record players were not yet around, the most popular musics in America are English ballads and Italian opera music.

1800-1900 Stephen Collins Foster becomes America's first important composer. His 200+ songs of memorable, simple text and melody include "Oh! Susanna" and "My Old Kentucky Home."

1920-1930 The American music industry is dominated by the sounds coming out of a lower Manhattan area of New York known as Tin Pan Alley. Broadway musicals, vaudeville performances, and dance orchestras popularize the works of George and Ira Gershwin and Richard Rodgers and Oscar Hammerstein.

1935-1945 Known as the Big Band Era, this time period brings fame to the likes of Benny Goodman and others who borrow much from the style of black jazz orchestras.

1945-1955 Gospel, country, rhythm and blues, boogie woogie, and doo-wop styles dominate the popular music scene.

1954-1959 The era known as the Golden Age of Rock and Roll lasts only five years. It begins when Alan Freed coins the term rock 'n' roll and Bill Haley's "Rock Around the Clock" becomes the first rock and roll hit song. Electric guitars come into vogue, and Elvis Presley, Buddy Holly, Chuck Berry, and many others rise to fame singing songs with teenage themes including love, freedom, and identity issues.

1960-1970 The British invasion takes America by surprise as the Beatles become enormously famous. Folk music, psychedelic rock, and hard rock become mainstream. Large-scale rock festivals promote popular music. Some popular songs have political rather than teenage themes.

1970-1980 Superstar rock groups, including Fleetwood Mac, The Rolling Stones, and Chicago dominate pop music. Punk rock, funk, and reggae appear in reaction against the commercialism of mainstream rock.

1980-1990 The compact disk revives a slowing pop music economy. Michael Jackson's *Thriller* album becomes the biggest selling album in history. Heavy metal bands and world beat music claim a portion of pop music sales.

1990-Beyond Major record companies continue to look to independent labels for new trends and talent. Rap, techno, alternative, grunge, hip-hop, and acid rock all make use of new technology while the lo-fi movement reflects the rockabilly sounds of the 1970s.

Superstars

Choose five of the popular music artists and/or groups listed on this page and write a one-paragraph summary of the work of each selected artist. Be certain your paragraph includes information on the time the group or artist was popular, a few of the songs the group or artist is known for, the style of popular music the group or artist records in, styles and artists who have influenced the artist or group, and any other interesting facts you might find.

Fats Domino

Eric Clapton

Pat Boone

Jimi Hendrix

Bo Diddley

Bill Haley

Carole King

The Supremes

Jerry Lee Lewis

Neil Sedaka

Smokey Robinson

Buddy Holly

David Bowie

The Temptations

The Beach Boys

The Platters

Bob Dylan

Stevie Wonder

Chuck Berry

T-Bone Walker

The Rolling Stones

Elvis Costello

Janis Joplin

Ice-T

Elton John

James Taylor

Michael Jackson

The Grateful Dead

The Eagles

Blood, Sweat, and Tears

Aerosmith

The Bee Gees

Led Zeppelin

Fleetwood Mac

Blondie

Little Richard

Talking Heads

M. C. Hammer

Bob Marley

Sly and the Family Stone

Bruce Springsteen

David Byrne

Paul Simon

Mikhail Gorbachev

When Mikhail Gorbachev assumed the leadership of the Communist Party in the USSR in 1985, he intended to reform that nation's economic system, reduce nuclear arms, and create a more open political climate. He did not anticipate restructuring all of Eastern Europe, dramatically altering the balance of world powers, or embarking upon a speaking career in defense of global environmental concerns.

Gorbachev was raised on a collective farm in Russia and groomed to assume power in the Communist Party. As a young man, he held several posts within the party, and in 1980 he became the youngest member of the Politburo. Yet as soon as Mikhail Gorbachev became head of the USSR, he began to introduce sweeping reforms that almost seemed to contradict the principles of communism. He decentralized the economy and democratized his party. He allowed free elections and was chosen president of his country. His determination to end the cold war and allow Soviet-bloc countries new freedoms earned Gorbachev the Nobel Peace Prize in October of 1990.

Yet his swift reforms caused hard-line Communists to stage an unsuccessful coup in August of 1991, and by the end of that same year, Gorbachev had resigned from both the Communist party and the president's position. By December of 1991, the USSR had voted itself out of existence, Soviet-bloc countries had declared their independence, and Gorbachev had started a new career. Having already greatly influenced the world by causing the restructuring of Eastern Europe and the end of the cold war, Gorbachev then turned his attention to what he called a "current crisis of civilization" that threatens all of life on earth. Mikhail Gorbachev founded Green Cross International and addresses forums around the globe in an attempt to get human beings to see our place within nature rather than separate from it before it is too late.

Which of Gorbachev's two missions do you see as the most important? Why?

_____

_____

International Green Cross

In 1992 Mikhail Gorbachev founded an organization called the International Green Cross that promotes sustainable development and environmental awareness. Mr. Gorbachev believes that humankind must begin to think of itself as a part of nature rather than the rulers of nature if people are to continue to populate this planet. Why are each of the following situations (which Mr. Gorbachev attempts to make people aware of) a threat to the survival of humankind? Write your answers in complete sentences. The first one has been done for you.

1. SITUATION: Nations all over the globe are developing market system economies.
   WHY IT IS A PROBLEM: <u>Market systems depend on selling more and more goods. Therefore, advertisements are designed to make the public desire more, better, bigger, and faster products now with no regard for future consequences of mass production. The result is the planet is stripped of its natural resources faster than they can be regenerated.</u>

2. SITUATION: The world's population is growing at an unprecedented rate.
   WHY IT IS A PROBLEM: _____

3. SITUATION: There exists no international environmental legal code.
   WHY IT IS A PROBLEM: _____

4. SITUATION: Natural and social scientists do not work together on global issues.
   WHY IT IS A PROBLEM: _____

5. SITUATION: People live according to the laws of nations rather than those of nature.
   WHY IT IS A PROBLEM: _____

6. SITUATION: Centuries' old moral principles are not applied to today's societies.
   WHY IT IS A PROBLEM: _____

The Earth Charter

Mikhail Gorbachev suggests that an "earth charter" needs to be created to provide the world with an international environmental legal code. "Rules" dictated by the charter might include such statements as "A nation's excess agricultural products must be shared with less fortunate nations" or "A nation's production level must respect the earth's regenerative limitations." Create international environmental codes of your own and write them in complete sentences below.

RULE ONE: _____

_____

RULE TWO: _____

_____

RULE THREE: _____

_____

RULE FOUR: _____

_____

RULE FIVE: _____

_____

RULE SIX: _____

_____

RULE SEVEN: _____

_____

RULE EIGHT: _____

_____

RULE NINE: _____

_____

RULE TEN: _____

_____

Mother Teresa

If your homework assignment tonight required you to name 50 people who have greatly influenced history, you would likely end up with a list of kings and presidents, war heroes, inventors, politicians, and reformers. Most people who have changed the world have done so in big ways, with broad strokes. They have changed public policies, initiated world wars, affected the balance of global powers, and introduced ideas or inventions that have altered how society thinks and operates.

Mother Teresa did no such things. She dictated no major shift in politics or economics. She ended no military conflict. She initiated no important reforms. Mother Teresa, rather, changed the world one seemingly insignificant person at a time.

In the autumn of 1948, this Roman Catholic nun, Sister Teresa, exited the sheltered and beautiful grounds of the private high school and convent in which she taught and lived, and entered the streets of Calcutta, India. Owning nothing more than two saris, a wash bucket, and prayer books, she gave of herself to the poorest of the poor—a population she considered the embodiment of Christ. While politicians and social reformers preached about the needs of the downtrodden, Mother Teresa addressed them. She established shelters for lepers, abandoned children, homeless families, and the lonely dying poor of India. She founded the Missionaries of Charity and taught other nuns to care for the needy. She raised funds for the creation of new hospitals, hospices, and shelters throughout the world. She persuaded the rich and the famous to contribute to her causes. But mostly, Mother Teresa cared for one person at a time—nursing the wounds of a leper, holding the hands of a dying Hindu, or singing a song with an abandoned child. According to Mother Teresa, no food, no medicine, and no political reforms can cure the feeling that one is unwanted. Only a loving heart can lessen the burden of that disease.

Which creates a more significant change: political reform resulting in law and policy changes or the tending to the needs of one individual at a time? _____

_____

_____

One Needy Soul at a Time

Mother Teresa is not the only person who has taken the approach of loving one person at a time in an effort to make the world a better place. Use an encyclopedia to help you match the humanitarians listed on the left with their accomplishments listed on the right. The first one has been done for you.

__F__ 1. Albert Schweitzer

_____ 2. Father Flanagan

_____ 3. Father Damien

_____ 4. Florence Nightingale

_____ 5. Clara Barton

_____ 6. Janusz Korczak

_____ 7. Harriet Tubman

A. This man served as a missionary to the lepers of Molokai, Hawaii, helping them build homes and plant crops even after contracting leprosy himself.

B. This "Angel of the Battlefield" assisted injured soldiers during three different wars including the Spanish-American war, which took place when she was 73 years old.

C. Following her own escape from slavery, this woman made 19 journeys back into the South to lead 300 more slaves to freedom in Canada.

D. This man opened a home and school for homeless and delinquent boys.

E. This woman served as a field nurse during the Crimean War.

F. This doctor introduced modern medicine to the people of the Congo region in Africa and cared for the area's sick animals as well.

G. This director of an orphanage in Poland was killed with his children during World War II, although he was offered his life if he would separate from his wards.

You Can Make a Difference

Young people often doubt that their efforts can make a difference in the world. However, there are many things that you can do to improve the quality of life for yourself, your classmates, and your community. In groups of four or five, choose at least one of the activities listed below to accomplish. You may choose to complete your project in a week or a month, or you may wish to continue it for the entire school year.

Our group will pick up trash on school grounds.

Our group will collect canned foods for a local food bank.

Our group will collect blankets and coats for a local shelter.

Our group will organize a concert for a local nursing home.

Our group will decorate local businesses with artwork.

Our group will plant flowers on school grounds.

Our group will write notes of appreciation to local civic groups, such as garden clubs and historical societies, who work to improve the quality of life in our community.

Our group will help decorate the school for holidays.

Our group will volunteer time in the classes of younger students.

Our group will collect needed supplies for a local human needs center.

Our group will collect old clothes and household items and take them to an area Goodwill center.

Our group will demonstrate respect and responsibility to the younger students who look up to us.

Our group will foster friendly relations in the classroom.

Our group will raise money for a local shelter or charity.

Answer Key

Reflecting on Glass page 3
1. C
2. E
3. I
4. A
5. D
6. B
7. F
8. H
9. J
10. G

Shaping Up page 4
1. Casting—3000 B.C.
2. Core Technique— 1500 B.C.
3. Glassblowing—50 B.C.
4. Crown Process—Sometime after the second century A.D.
5. Pressing—eighth to fourteenth centuries A.D.
6. Old Style Glass Rolling—Late 1600s
7. Drawing—Early 1900s
8. Pilkington's Process of New Style Rolling—1950s

I'm Sorry, Did I Wake You? page 9
1. Better wait a few hours for your investor to get into his office. It is 4:00 a.m. in Sydney.
2. I hope you are awake. It is 1:00 in the afternoon in Nebraska.
3. Your classmate is mistaken. Although Maine and Manaus, Brazil, are hundreds of miles apart, they are both in the same time zone. If you call your friend in the afternoon from your home in Maine, it will be in the afternoon in your friend's home as well.

Keeping Time page 10
1. Graham's Deadbeat
2. Chronographs
3. Coiled Springs
4. Water Clock
5. Atomic Clock
6. Mechanical Clock
7. Pillar and Scroll Clock
8. Liquid Crystal Display
9. Electric Clocks
10. Pendulum
11. Light-Emitting Diode
12. Quartz-Crystal Clock

Ka-boom! page 13
1. D
2. C
3. D
4. A
5. B
6. C
7. B
8. D
9. B
10. D
11. C
12. A

The Printing Press page 14
2000 B.C. Signet Stones
A.D. 150 Wood Block Printing
1450 Johannes Gutenberg's Printing Press
1814 Steam-Powered Press
1863 Web-Fed Newspaper Press
1886 Typesetting Machine
1950 Phototypesetting Machine
1978 Desktop Publishing

The Printed Word page 15
1. Cereal Box
2. Newspaper
3. Calendar
4. Computer Printer
5. Encyclopedia
6. Library Book
7. Sweatshirt
8. Poster
9. Bumper Stickers
10. Stop Sign
11. Principal Parking Sign
12. Copy Machine
13. Clock
14. Parking Ticket
15. Detention Slip

Modern Printing Techniques page 16
1. D
2. A
3. G
4. B
5. C
6. E
7. F
8. H

Out to Sea page 18
1. A *gyrocompass* is a gyroscope that acts like a compass and is unaffected by magnetic variations. It is used aboard ships and airplanes for navigational purposes.
2. A *sextant* uses one fixed mirror and one moving mirror to superimpose the images of two objects as it measures the angle between an observer and a celestial body in determining a ship's longitude and latitude.
3. *LORAN* is a navigational system that compares the arrival time of two pairs of radio transmissions in pinpointing an aircraft pilot's location.
4. The *Doppler Effect* represents changes in wavelength that accompany moves in a wave in relation to an observer; the changes are helpful to sailors and pilots who make use of systems of navigation using artificial satellites today.
5. *Reckoning* refers to the calculating of a ship's position at sea.
6. A *chronometer* is an extremely accurate timepiece used for navigational purposes.
7. An *altimeter* is an instrument used in measuring the height of aircraft.
8. *Radar* helps ships and aircraft determine their position by detecting the time it takes for a radio wave to travel from one antenna to another and back.
9. The *Global Positioning System* consists of 24 satellites that assist aircraft, ships, and rockets in navigation.
10. *Guidance and control systems* that are being perfected in space flight rely on electromagnetic information to allow most maneuvers in space to be conducted from the ground.
11. The *log* becomes the daily record of a ship or aircraft's progress.
12. A *Mercator Projection* is a projected map that compensates for the globe's curves so that a navigator can chart a course on paper.

Cause and Effect page 21
1. D
2. G
3. E
4. B
5. L
6. C
7. A
8. F
9. J
10. H
11. I
12. K

All Aboard page 22
1. False—Trains were used for the transport of goods and passengers 25 years after the construction of the first practical locomotive.
2. True
3. False—The United States was connected coast to coast by railroads by 1869.
4. True
5. False—Steamboats operated on the Mississippi River.
6. False—Steam locomotives were used in the United States for more than 100 years.
7. True

Arms of the Automotive Industry page 24
Vehicle and Safety Regulations
   Automotive Insurance Employees
   Highway Patrol Officers
   DMV Employees
   Driving School Instructors
   Meteorologists
   Traffic and Road Condition Reporters
   Emissions Controls Employees
   Paramedics
   Lobbyists, Congresspeople, and Auto Law Makers
Auto Design and Construction
   Computer Engineers
   Automotive Factory Employees
   Automobile Engineers and Designers
   Steel, Plastic, Glass, and Rubber Factory Employees

Road Maintenance
 Infrastructure Engineers
 Road Construction and Maintenance Employees
Auto Repairs and Maintenance
 Car Wash Employees
 Oil Refinery Employees
 Gas Station Attendants
 Mechanics and Body Shop Employees
Transportation of Products and People
 Truck Drivers
 Bus and Taxi Drivers
Auto Rentals and Sales
 New and Used Car Dealers
 Advertisement Agency Employees
 Car Importers and Exporters
 Auto Rental Agency Employees
Other Jobs That Use Vehicles
 Race Car Drivers
 Farmers and Ranchers
 Rural Postal Carriers

A World of Plastic page 27

1.	F	7.	D
2.	C	8.	G
3.	A	9.	J
4.	I	10.	E
5.	B	11.	K
6.	L	12.	H

Silicon City page 31

1. A *microprocessor* is a single chip that performs all of the logic and arithmetic functions of a small computer.
2. A *central processing unit* encompasses millions of electrical components on a single silicon circuit board to perform the calculations and comparisons necessary to control processing in a computer. A computer's CPU is often a microprocessor.
3. *Integrated circuits*, also known as microchips, refer to tiny electrical circuits that perform a specific function.
4. *RAM* refers to random access memory chips that contain numerous transistors which provide a computer with its memory.
5. A *microcontroller* used in VCRs, video games, and automobiles is like a complete computer on a single chip.
6. A *semiconductor* is a substance such as silicon which conducts electricity at a rate between that of conductors and insulators. Integrated circuits are made from semiconductors.
7. A *transistor* is an integrated circuit that operates like an on-off switch.
8. Because microchips are so small and their wiring so precise, a single speck of dust can contaminate an entire batch of chips being created. Therefore, the well-filtered, nearly dust-free rooms where microchips are made are called *clean rooms*.
9. *Buses* are sets of hardware lines used to carry information throughout a chip and an entire computer.
10. *Microcomputers* are small computers used in businesses, schools, and homes. They are also called personal computers, or PCs.

Six-Million Dollar Man page 32

The answers to this exercise are self-explanatory. The purpose of labeling all of the body parts listed is to demonstrate to students visually how extensively the use of silicone is in the creation of synthetic prosthetic devices.

To Market, To Market . . . page 34

The sequential ordering of the steps involved in processing and distributing foods is 2-5-6-1-3-4.

1.	C	6.	B
2.	F	7.	J
3.	I	8.	H
4.	A	9.	D
5.	E	10.	G

Raking the Muck page 35

1.	Edwin Markham	6.	Ida M. Tarbell
2.	Samuel McClure	7.	Harvey Washington Wiley
3.	Thomas Lawson	8.	Upton Sinclair
4.	Teddy Roosevelt	9.	Ray Stannard Baker
5.	Lincoln Steffens		

As the Wheel Turns page 38

1. An *applied force* is the force or energy that is exerted on a machine.
2. A *pulley* is a simple machine consisting of a rope lapped over a grooved wheel for the purpose of changing the direction of an applied force.
3. *Magnitude* refers to the size or extent of a force.
4. A *wheel and axle* consists of a large and small wheel that share a center so that a force exerted on the large wheel is multiplied in the small wheel.
5. *Gears* are toothed wheels that interlock to transmit motion.
6. The *mechanical advantage* of a machine defines how effective the machine is by dividing the output force by the input force.
7. *Output force* refers to the energy the machine exerts.
8. *Input force* refers to the energy the person puts into the machine.

Simple Machines page 39

1.	Lever	7.	Inclined plane
2.	Wheel and axle	8.	Wheel and axle
3.	Inclined plane	9.	Inclined plane
4.	Lever	10.	Wheel and axle
5.	Pulley	11.	Pulley
6.	Lever		

CU page 41

The symbols in the story stand for the following words:

I	newspaper
son	bat
balloon	ring
airplane	telephone
smile	too
wave(d)	sea
fan	

ABC's page 42

1.	A	6.	M
2.	E	7.	T
3.	H	8.	I
4.	P	9.	N
5.	B	10.	S

The Concept of Free Trade page 44

(questions based on the reading)

The advantages of free trade and a global economic system include the ability for nations to produce what they are best at producing and to trade for those items that other countries produce best without restrictions. A global economy makes it possible for banks and businesses to expand worldwide.

Although the quoted advantages of exercising protected trading are probably valid, a nation that sets high tariffs and stringent governmental restrictions on trading runs the risk of facing retaliation from other nations.

Definitions:

Tariffs are duties imposed on imported goods.
Mercantilism is an economic system that suggests that a country should maintain a surplus of exports over imports to maintain wealth.
A *surplus* refers to the amount of a given thing that is left over.
Exports are items that a country sells to another country.
Imports are items that a country buys from another country.
Natural resources are resources from nature that are found in a given nation.

Free trade refers to the concept of unregulated trading in the absence of tariffs, quotas, and other restrictions.
The *General Agreement on Tariffs and Trades* is an agreement signed by 23 nations following World War II stating that signatories would promote free trade and remove some trading tariffs and restrictions.
The *World Trade Organization* replaced GATT in 1995.
The *North American Free Trade Agreement* is a treaty that was signed by Mexico, Canada, and the United States in 1994 stating that the three countries would gradually remove trading tariffs.
The *European Union* promotes cooperation among several participating countries in matters of trade and other social and economic areas.

The European Community   page 45
1. no   8. yes
2. yes   9. yes
3. yes   10. yes
4. no   11. yes
5. yes
6. yes
7. no—the council has an advisory role only, no vote

The Men Behind the Movement   page 50
1. D   5. E
2. C   6. F
3. B   7. A
4. G

Language of the Stars   page 51
1. Milky Way   9. comet
2. galaxy   10. universe
3. nebula   11. meteorite
4. planet   12. black hole
5. quasar   13. star
6. asteroid   14. orbit
7. solar system   15. eclipse
8. telescope

Name That Instrument   page 53
Instrument #1 is a xylophone of the percussion family.
Instrument #2 is an organ of the keyboard family.
Instrument #3 is a tuba of the wind family.
Instrument #4 is an oboe of the wind family.
Instrument #5 is a lute of the string family.
Instrument #6 is a sitar of the string family.

Making Music   page 54

The Concept of Inalienable Rights   page 56
Absolutism—a form of government which vests all power in a single leader
Divine Right—the belief that a ruler receives his authority to govern from God
Inalienable Rights—the concept that all people are entitled to certain rights and freddoms simply by virtue of their being human beings

Fighters for Freedom and Equality   page 57
1. John Wilkes   7. Jeremy Bentham
2. Montesquieu   8. James Madison
3. Plato   9. Jean-Jacques Rousseau
4. John Locke   10. Voltaire
5. Thomas Jefferson   11. Socrates
6. Thomas Hobbes   12. Thomas Paine

Dreamers and Inventors in Manufacturing   page 59
1. A   5. B
2. C   6. E
3. H   7. G
4. F   8. D

Extraction, Alteration, Microprocessors, and Feedback Loops
pages 60 and 61
1. Computer-aided design   11. Modem automation
2. Feedback loop   12. Artificial intelligence
3. Detroit automation   13. Robots
4. Transfer machine   14. Cottage industry
5. CAM   15. FMS
6. Microprocessor   16. Interchangeable parts
7. Assembly line   17. Mass production
8. Extraction   18. Factory
9. Alteration   19. Cybernetics
10. Assembly   20. Mechanization

Branches of Psychology   page 63
Psychoanalysis is a form of psychotherapy based on the theories of Freud, which suggest that an exploration of unconscious motives can assist a person in changing behaviors.
Experimental Psychology refers to the use of experiments to better understand memory, perception, thinking, and learning processes.
Clinical Psychology is concerned with the use of counseling and drugs to help patients improve the quality of their lives.
Social Psychology addresses how people's attitudes, emotions, judgments, and behaviors are influenced by social input.
Behavioral Psychology focuses on how people change as a result of experience. It is an experimentally based branch of psychology that attempts to answer such questions as how people learn and form habits.
Physiological Psychology studies the nervous and circulatory systems and examines how the brain and body function together. Technological advances make this a rapidly growing field in psychology.
Industrial Psychology applies the principles of psychology to concerns of the workplace.
School Psychology focuses on career guidance, educational testing, conflict resolution, social and esteem issues, and individual and group counseling among school children.
Psychiatry is a branch of medicine concerned with psychiatric disorders that cause people pain, cause them to lose touch with reality, or cause them to act in antisocial ways.
Sports Psychology is concerned with how individuals react in competitive situations.
Cybernetics studies how people and machines process information.
Psycholinguistics looks at the role attention, memory, and language play in learning processes.
Psychological Testing is used to predict success in school or on the job, as well as to assess personality traits and attitudes. Constructing and interpreting effective psychological tests is a complete branch of psychology in and of itself.
Abnormal Psychology classifies and defines behaviors that deviate from the norm.
Developmental Psychology is the study of how behaviors in general change from infancy to old age.

Totalitarian Time Line   page 69
1924-1943 Benito Mussolini, Italy
1929-1953 Joseph Stalin, USSR
1933-1945 Adolf Hitler, Germany
1934-1976 Mao Tse-Tung, China
1948-1994 Kim II Sung, North Korea
1970-Present Hafez al-Assad, Syria
1979-Present Saddam Hussein, Iraq

Making Sense of Modern Art   page 72
1. Jackson Pollock   6. Grandma Moses
2. Willem de Kooning   7. Pablo Picasso
3. Salvador Dali   8. Mark Rothko
4. Henri Matisse   9. Andy Warhol
5. Kenneth Noland

Computer Connections
page 75

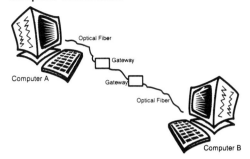

Optical Fiber

Computer A

Gateway

Gateway

Optical Fiber

Computer B

Internet Access
page 76
Sites will vary, but some include the following:
1. www.law.cornell.edu/constitution/constitutionoverview
2. www.nando.net/triguide/almanac/legfiled/usdistrict
3. asiatravelnet.com/thailand/map
4. news.lycos.com/headlines/topnews/default.asp
5. www.butterball.com
6. www.lycos.com (click on Yellow Pages, follow prompts)
7. weather.lycos.com
8. www.traveleasy.com
9. pages.prodigy.com/psykobrain/roald_main
10. groty.simplenet.com
11. www.asap.unimelb.edu.au
12. www.cpec.ca.gov

Greek Influence
page 79
1. B
2. E
3. C
4. G
5. D
6. A
7. F
8. H

From Cornfield to Battlefield
pages 82 and 83
1. William the Conqueror confused the French-English lines of nationality by being a French ruler of England. His ancestors continued to fight over boundaries.
2. 19
3. Two years
4. (a) The commander does not trust that a 16-year-old girl who reports hearing voices that spell out a mission for her can help much in a war that has found no resolution in 100 years.
(b) The commander accepts the advice of one of his trusted soldiers who speaks on behalf of Joan during her second visit and gives her the escort she requests.
5. After
6. Joan of Arc is accused of witchcraft, for wearing boys' clothing, and answering to God before the church.
7. Joan united soldiers and saved her country from English rule. She turned the tide on the Hundred Years' War at the battle in Orleans.
8. 1429
9. Before the closing of the Hundred Years' War, French citizens felt more allegiance to regions than to their nation as a whole. Therefore, some regions of France fought on the side of the English during the conflict. Through Joan of Arc's efforts the people felt more allegiance to their country.
10. Joan of Arc has been the subject of many art and literature projects including works by the author Mark Twain, the sculptor Anna Vaughn Hyatt, the playwright George Bernard Shaw, and the composer Arthur Honegger.

The Power of Personality
page 85
2. Benefit—His hunger for power made Napoleon willing to declare himself emperor and demand the reforms he believed in.
Hindrance—His hunger for power made him storm European powers that could eventually beat him by uniting together in anger against him.
3. Benefit—His ability to charm people convinced them to go along with his plans.

Hindrance—His ability to charm angered people who learned they were being manipulated for Napoleon's personal goals only.
4. Benefit—Napoleon's inability to relax drove him to achieve. He even instituted political, legal, and democratic reforms on the island of Elba, where he was supposed to be a powerless exiled ex-monarch.
Hindrance—Napoleon's inability to relax could have contributed to the stomach cancer that eventually killed him.
5. Benefit—Napoleon's loyalty to his family added to his popularity as it softened the hearts of the public, who saw him as a common and caring man.
Hindrance—The many relatives Napoleon appointed to important posts in France and in conquered lands were not always the most qualified for the job.
6. Benefit—Napoleon was his own publicist. He carefully orchestrated the publicity of his victories and celebrated his rule with elaborate ceremonies. He created a cult of followers who continue to praise him today.
Hindrance—Some historians doubt the truth of certain stories because Napoleon was so famous for promoting himself. Although Napoleon wanted to be seen as having founded a European state in the form of a "federation of free people" based on the principles fought for in the French Revolution, some historians contend he was nothing more than an authoritarian tyrant.
7. Benefit—Both Napoleon's military conquests and his political reforms can be attributed to the fact that he was never satisfied.
Hindrance—His inability to be satisfied drove Napoleon to try to control more than he had the power to control in the end.
8. Benefit—His drive to achieve made Napoleon able to accomplish a lot in a little time.
Hindrance—Napoleon's drive to achieve made him unable to know when to exercise caution.

Boy Genius
page 88
1. False
2. False—Although he did compose over 600 pieces of music, Mozart died of kidney disease at the young age of 35.
3. True and False—He was quite famous in Europe during his lifetime, but Mozart was also criticized by some contemporaries for breaking away from traditional styles and rejected by some monarchs who did not care for his irreverent personality.
4. True—Johann Christian Bach, by the way, was one of Johann Sebastian Bach's 20 children.
5. True
6. True
7. True
8. True
9. False—Although chamber composer of the Viennese court was one of the positions he held during his lifetime, Mozart continued to do as much traveling and engage in as many varied assignments in his adulthood as he did as a child.
10. True

A Few Notes About Music
page 89
1. *Classical music* refers to European music of the late eighteenth and early nineteenth centuries.
2. *Baroque music* is extremely elaborate European music of the 1600s or 1700s.
3. An *opera*, one of the most respected forms of music in the day of Mozart, is a play set to music.
4. A *chant* is a monotonic melody in which several words are sung on a single note.
5. *Chamber music* is composed to be performed in a small concert hall.
6. A *serenade* is a musical performance dedicated to a person or a person's honor.
7. *Folk music* originates with the common people of a region.
8. A *symphony* is a large-scale piece of music written for an entire orchestra.
9. A *minuet* is music written to accompany the seventeenth-century French dance of the same name.

10. A *sonata* is a piece of music written in three or four movements for one or two instruments.
11. A *concerto* is a piece of music written for an entire orchestra that features one or more solo sections.
12. A *requiem* is the musical composition of a Catholic mass for the dead.

Lucretia Mott Accomplished a Lot   page 91
1. Lucretia Mott was an eloquent speaker.
2. Lucretia Mott was a gracious hostess and great cook.
3. At the beginning of her crusade, Lucretia Mott was not always well received.
4. Lucretia Mott was always a family person.

Lucretia's Contemporaries   page 92
1. William Lloyd Garrison
2. Sojourner Truth
3. Charles Dickens
4. The Hutchinsons
5. Elizabeth Stanton
6. Susan B. Anthony
7. Ralph Waldo Emerson
8. James Mott
9. Abraham Lincoln
10. Lucy Stone
11. Frederick Douglass
12. Ernestine Rose

The Rockefeller Clan   page 94
1. D
2. E
3. A
4. G
5. B
6. F
7. C

The Rockefeller Foundation   page 95
Agricultural Sciences: B, K, O, S, U
Arts and Humanities: A, E, G, N, Q, R
Population and Health Sciences: C, D, F, M, P
Equal Opportunities: H, I J, L, P, T

Norman Borlaug: He's Made a Difference: Is It a Positive One?   page 97
1. He won the prize for cultivating high yield crops and introducing modern farming techniques to developing nations thereby saving countless lives from starvation.
2. Mr. Borlaug's opponents contend that the availability of more food allows for increased population growth. Mr. Borlaug cites research that suggests the opposite. In fact, a 1997 issue of the *Atlantic Monthly* about Mr. Borlaug contends that his high-yield farming methods are responsible for the fact that food production has expanded faster than population growth in all parts of the world except the sub-Saharan in recent years.
3. Supporters of the revolution point out the lives and forests that have been saved by introducing high-yield farming methods to developing nations. They contend that the use of chemical fertilizers to replace soil components allows for the most effective production of food, since manure use relies on the presence of livestock that eat grains which could go to humans. They remind opponents that the revolution supports low-pesticide plant breeds and that pesticides, not fertilizers, are highly detrimental to the environment. Opponents believe more available food encourages population growth and do not like the idea of introducing chemicals to places that are yet unadulterated by their use in their own farming techniques.
4. Personal opinion.

Understanding Agriculture   page 98
1. fertilizer
2. world food supply
3. chemical
4. cultivate
5. genetic engineering
6. pesticide
7. high-yield crops
8. integrated pest management
9. dwarf wheat

Chain of Events   page 101
The sequence of events should be numbered as follows:
4-1-7-10-2-8-5-3-6-9-12-11

Steadfastness in Truth   page 106
1. C
2. B
3. E
4. F
5. D
6. A
7. H
8. G

A Full Life   page 107
Mohandas Gandhi was loved by millions.
Facts 1, 10, and 12
Mohandas Gandhi achieved change.
Facts 7 and 8
Mohandas Gandhi lived a simple life.
Facts 3 and 4
Mohandas Gandhi led by example.
Facts 2, 5, and 6
Mohandas Gandhi sometimes surprised and even angered followers.
Facts 9 and 11

We're Not There Yet   page 109
2. Including economic factors in the equation for setting safe levels of pesticide use means sometimes legally accepting damaging levels of pesticide usage.
3. Children are most affected by chemicals and so should be included in research about the effects of pesticides on humans.
4. Pesticides that are known to be harmful continue to be used for long periods of time because of the lengthy process involved in getting them removed from the market.
5. The fact that chemicals used in combination are often more harmful than those used in isolation is not addressed by research that focuses on individual pesticides only.
6. Since it is not easy to prove beyond a doubt that pesticides are responsible for human disease due to the fact that so many factors are involved in human disease rates, pesticides continue to be used even when rates of cancer or reproductive problems rise in a given area where pesticide usage is prevalent.
7. The true safety of a pesticide is not the only factor considered in deciding whether it should be used or banned.

International Green Cross   page 115
2. Already the earth does not provide enough fresh drinking water for all of its inhabitants. Available land and farming techniques cannot keep up with the nutritional needs of an unchecked population.
3. Because no international environmental code dictates the environmental decisions of nations, countries make decisions based on their own immediate political and social interests. This is an artificial and short-sighted way to make decisions about global issues, since environmental concerns have no borders and pleasing today's voters can be devastating to future generations.
4. Because social and political leaders do not work with natural scientists, real concerns strongly voiced by the scientific community have gone unheeded. Very little progress has been made in saving the planet since the Earth Summit of 1992. Even though scientists' statements seemed to be taken seriously, political issues have stood in the way of progress.
5. Mikhail Gorbachev suggests that humankind's tendency to live according to our own laws while neglecting the laws of nature will result in our demise unless we bring this problem into check soon.
6. Mr. Gorbachev suggests that both Christian and Buddhist values that emphasize moral responsibility and a connection with nature and one another need to be remembered in the creation of a new value system based on nature rather than nations.

One Needy Soul at a Time   page 118
1. F
2. D
3. A
4. E
5. B
6. G
7. C